TABLE OF CONTENTS

THANKS TO

Simon Lereng Wilmont and Jes Larsen for the lovely photos.

Marie Monrad Graunbøl/Revolver for the introductory texts for each decade and for the invaluable help with styling at the photo sessions.

Pernille Damgaard Jensen/Pilo Organic Hair for fantastic hair styling and make-up.

Nvey Eco/make-up.

Steen and René/AVITV for loan of the photo studio.

Trice Tomsen/Elite Models.

My patient and lovely models: Elin Mildrid Keiding Lindholm, Fanny Kiwimaki, Malin Højegaard, Pernille Bæk Nielsen, Sara Maria Dyrberg and William Hidalgo Munthe.

Nees and Schelde, Divaen and Krudtuglen, Potz Braunlein, Sungifu, Min Mingus and Melanie's Masker for lending clothing and accessories.

Marianne Isager for technical help and great support.

Annette Ross for expert corrections.

Valerie Collart/Collart and Brink for such fine retouching.

Klematis Publishers for the invitation for writing this book and being so good to work with.

And, last but not least, a huge thanks to my expert knitters: Kristen Ravn, Karin Kainhofer, Lone Møss, Louise Pløhn and Ulla Bohlin.

FOREWORD

Strikketøj has been inspired by the shifting styles of the 20th century—from the economic optimism and extravagant use of luxury materials in the early 1900s to androgynous grunge and the rebellious proclamations of the new sounds from music's underground. No matter what period, I've tried to capture the spirit of an era for my inspiration rather than attempting to present historically correct shaping, colors, or patterns. Instead, you'll find a line of modern interpretations of the dominant trends through a century, as fashion conveys its own history about war and peace, woman's emancipation, and cultural disturbances, rebellion and change.

A wide range of different knitting techniques has been used for the models in this book. Many of them can be worked by beginners because I most prefer techniques that are easy to learn – and, even though the stitches look complicated, knitting them soon becomes a relaxing and fun process.

For beginners, there is a help section at the back of the book where, aided by Åse Lund Jensen's fine drawings, I have described the basic techniques necessary for you to start knitting.

All the patterns list the materials and gauge. It is important that the gauge be correct, so, it is a good idea to begin by making a gauge swatch. If the gauge isn't correct, try again with larger or smaller needles.

It is also very important for the final result that the recommended yarn be used—it just doesn't pay to use bad quality yarn when you are going to spend so many hours working on a project. It should go without saying that you do not need to follow the patterns slavishly. This is really what makes hand knitting so exciting. You can change the measurements and colors and open up the possibilities for creating your own totally unique knitted garments.

All the best!
Helga Isager

1900s

Corsets were cinched ever more tightly around the waist and long powder-colored silk dresses draped heavily to the floor. At that time, young British ladies ready for marriage had delicate porcelain skin and upswept curls. They dressed immaculately in luxurious outfits bought in Paris at Rue de Paix number 7, the fashion house of Charles Worth, the father of haute couture. These privileged creatures danced to light salon music and recited poetry to their virtuous friends at tea parties under the watchful eyes of their mothers and governesses. An attractive woman was not just a shy beauty of good family but a generous hostess with an eye for every last detail. As noted in the epoch's popular magazine for young women, *The Lady's Realm:* "As soon as a visit is fixed, exact and extensive preparations must be made. Probably few outside our well-informed circle understand the requirements for these necessary arrangements." Etiquette was not something to be ignored. Chairs were reupholstered, plants brought in to the country house rooms, and the perfect stage for high society was created. La belle époque needed its women. While women were the flowers of the home, men's nature drove them to hitherto unseen daring. The first manned flying machine was regarded with awe when the brothers Wilbur and Orville Wright took off into the sky on 17 December 1903. In exactly 59 seconds men had done what was previously thought impossible. A new century had begun.

> At that time, young British ladies ready for marriage had delicate porcelain skin and upswept curls. They dressed immaculately in luxurious outfits bought in Paris at Rue de Paix number 7, the fashion house of Charles Worth, the father of haute couture

CARDIGAN WITH BELL EDGINGS

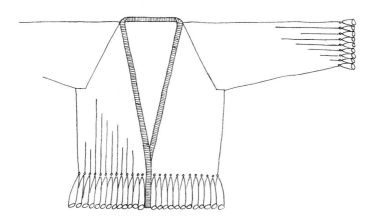

Sizes: S (M, L)

Measurements

Chest: 31½ (34¼, 37) in / 80 (87, 94) cm
Sleeve length from underarm: 11¼ (12, 12½) in / 28.5 (30.5, 31.5) cm
Body length below underarm: 12¾ (13½, 13¾) in / 32 (34, 35) cm
Armhole measured vertically to shoulder: 7½ (7½, 8) in / 19 (19, 20) cm

Yarn

250 (300, 350) g Isager Alpaca 2, color 015 (peach).

Notions: 59 in / 150 cm ribbon about ¾ in / 2 cm wide to match yarn.

Needles: US size 2.5 / 3 mm (straight and 40 in / 100 cm circular).

Gauge

30 sts (stretched slightly) and 40 rows in k1/p3 ribbing = 4 x 4 in / 10 x 10 cm.
Adjust needle size to obtain correct gauge if necessary.

The cardigan is worked back and forth beginning at lower edge.

BACK AND FRONT

With long circular, CO 264 (288, 312) sts and work bell edging as follows:

Row 1 (WS): K1, p1, k260 (284, 308), p1, k1.

Row 2 (RS): K2, p4, *CO 8 new sts, p4*. Rep * to * and end with k2 = 776 (848, 920) sts.

Row 3: K1, p1, k4, *p8, k4*. Rep * to * and end with p1, k1.

Row 4: K2, p4, *k8, p4*. Rep * to * and end with k2.

Repeat rows 3–4 until piece measures about 2½ in / 6 cm. End with a WS row.

Now begin decreases:

Row 1 (RS): K2, p4, *ssk, k4, k2tog, p4*. Rep * to * and end with k2.

Row 2: K1, p1, k4, *p6, k4*. Rep * to * and end with p1, k1.

Row 3: K2, p4, *ssk, k2, k2tog, p4*. Rep * to * and end with k2.

Row 4: K1, p1, k4, *p4, k4*. Rep * to * and end with p1, k1.

Row 5: K2, p4, *ssk, k2tog, p4*. Rep * to * and end with k2 = 392 (428, 464) sts rem.

Make a lace row next:

Row 6 (WS): k1, p1, *k1, k2tog, k1, p1, yo, p1*. Rep * to * and work last rep as: k1, k2tog, k1, p1, k1.

Row 7: K2, p4, *sl 1-k2tog-psso, p3*. Rep * to * and end with k2 = 264 (288, 312) sts rem.

Row 8: K1, p1, *k3, p1* Rep * to * and end with p1, k1.

Mark the 2 stockinette sts at each side. You will increase before/after each pair of side sts. Pm at both sides between the 16th and 17th (17th and 18th, 18th and 19th) bells as counted from front edge. *At the same time,* you will shape V-neck by dec inside the 2 outermost sts of each front edge.

Shaping Sides: Work in Rib pattern (k1, p3),

continuing pattern as set by row 8. On the first RS row inc with m1 (lift strand between 2 sts and knit into back loop) at each side of the marked side sts = work across to first marker, m1, sl marker, k2, sl marker, m1; work across to first marker on other side, m1, sl marker, k2, sl marker, m1 = 4 sts increased on row. Now there are 4 sts between the increases at the sides. Continue increasing the same way (before/after markers for paired side sts) on every 24th (26th, 26th) row a total of 4 times. Work the new sts into rib pattern.

At the same time, shape V-neck, which begins at the waist.

On the first RS row, ssk inside the 2 outermost sts of right front edge and end row with k2tog, k2 at left front edge. Work these decreases on every 6th row.

After the last increase at the sides, continue in pattern with V-neck shaping until piece measures 12¾ (13½, 13¾) in / 32 (34, 35) cm. Place the center 14 sts at each side on a holder and set body aside.

THREE-QUARTER LENGTH SLEEVES

With straight ndls, CO 80 (88, 96) sts and work Rows 1–4 of bell edging as for body of cardigan and then repeat rows 3 and 4 until piece measures about 1 in / 2.5 cm. Work rows 1–8 for decreases and lace and then work in ribbing as for body of sweater.

Next, on the first RS row, inc with m1 inside the 2 outermost (edge) sts at each side. Rep increase on every 12th row a total of 8 times = 96 (104, 112) sts. Work straight up without further shaping until ribbing measures 10¼ (11, 11½) in / 26 (28, 29) cm.

Place 7 sts at each side on a holder = 82 (90, 98) sts rem. Make sure that patterns on sleeves and back/front of body match. Set first sleeve aside while you make the other one the same way.

JOINING

Now place sleeves onto long circular with body, placing sleeves between gaps at front and back. Mark the 4 intersections for the raglan seam (= 1 st from the sleeve and 1 st from the body). The 4 x 2 marked sts are always worked in stockinette = knit on RS and purl on WS. On, alternately, every 2nd and 3rd row, k2tog (on RS) or p2tog (on WS) at each side of these marked seam sts (= 8 sts dec per dec row). To begin raglan: beg at right front edge, work until 2 sts before first marker, *k2tog, sl marker, k2, sl marker, k2tog*, work until 2 sts before next marker and rep * to * at each marked raglan line.

Work a total of 32 (32, 34) raglan dec rows.

At the same time, continue to decrease at front neck edges until no more sts remain for front pieces.

FINISHING

Steam press all the pieces lightly. Seam sleeves with mattress st and, with RS facing RS, join underarms with three-needle bind-off. With long circular and RS facing, pick up and knit sts all around front edges and neck. Pick up approximately 3 sts for every 4 rows. Make sure you have a multiple of 2 + 1. Beginning on WS, work 5 rows of k1, p1 ribbing (WS begins with p1). BO in ribbing on RS.

Thread ribbon through lace row at the waist.

1910s

Even on the day of embarkation, April 10, 1912, things were a little crazy. The gigantic luxury liner, the Titanic, had barely steamed out from the British port of Southampton on its maiden voyage to New York when the alarm sounded. A fire had broken out in one of the machine rooms and the crew had to rush there to put out the fire. But on the deck above they took no notice. Among the 2230 expectant passengers who had bought tickets to the long-awaited voyage on the impressive ship, were both poor emigrants crammed together in the third class and the adventurous wealthy who sipped champagne and toasted the progress of technology in the ship's luxurious salons. The world's richest man, the American hotelier John Jacob Astor and his pregnant wife, Madeleine were among the prominent guests. They were on their honeymoon, and, along with Molly Brown, the young daughter of a plutocrat, they

At midnight of April 14th, the Titanic rammed an iceberg which perforated the hull under the water line. A tray of freshly baked bread glided across the floor and the restaurant's porcelain china lightly clinked, while the orchestra played on

came aboard at the first stop of the trip in northern French town of Cherbourg. At midnight of April 14th, the Titanic rammed an iceberg which perforated the hull under the water line. A tray of freshly baked bread glided across the floor and the restaurant's porcelain china lightly clinked, while the orchestra played on. The bow of the top deck sunk just three hours later but Molly Brown and Madeleine Astor were among the fortunate who found places in the all too few lifeboats. A newspaper summary of the rescued listed John Jacob Astor as no. 124. His belongings: a gold watch, a pair of diamond cuff links, a bundle of cash, a ring and a thoroughly soaked notebook.

Soul Warmer

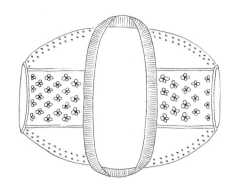
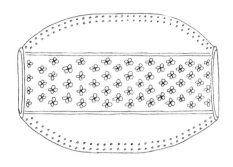

Sizes: S/M (M/L)

Measurements

Wingspan: 26 (27½) in / 66 (70) cm
Sleeve width, lower edge: 18¼ (21) in / 46 (53) cm
Sleeve width, top: 35½ (38½) in / 90 (98) cm

Yarn

150 (200) g Isager Alpaca 2, color 017 (curry)

Needles

US sizes 2.5 / 3 mm (16 and 24 in / 40 and 60 cm circulars) and US 4 / 3.5 mm (straight or 24 in / 60 cm circular).

Gauge

22 sts and 34 rows in bobble pattern on larger ndls = 4 x 4 in / 10 x 10 cm.
26 sts and 34 rows in stockinette on larger ndls = 4 x 4 in / 10 x 10 cm.
Adjust needle size to obtain correct gauge if necessary.

Bobbles

Knit alternately into front and back of st a total of 3 times = 6 sts into 1. Next, slip the 5th, 4th, 3rd, 2nd and 1st sts over the 6th.

Lace increase (lace inc)

Lift the strand between 2 sts to left ndl and knit into front and back of loop = 2 new sts (makes a small hole at that spot).

The soul warmer is worked across from sleeve to sleeve.

BACK

With larger ndls, CO 51 (59) sts and work as follows:

Row 1 (WS): K1, p7 (11), k2, sl 1 purlwise wyf (= 1 relief st), k29, sl 1 purlwise wyf, k2, p7 (11), k1.

Row 2: K8 (12), p2, k1 (= over relief st), p29, k1 (over relief st), p2, k8 (12).

Row 3: As for row 1.

Row 4: As for row 2.

Row 5: As for row 1.

Now begin the bobble pattern:

Row 6 (RS): K3, make a lace increase, k2, yo, k2tog, k1 (5), p2, k1, p5, bobble into next st, p5, bobble, p5, bobble, p5, bobble, p5, k1, p2, k1 (5), ssk, yo, k2, lace increase, k3 = 55 (63) sts.

Row 7: As for row 1, purling all the new sts.

Row 8: K10 (14), p2, k1, p4, (bobble, p1, bobble, p3) 4 times. End with p1, k1, p2, k10 (14).

Rows 9, 11, 13, 15, 17, 19, 21, 23, and 25: As for row 7 (don't forget to purl new sts).

Row 10: K10 (14), p2, k1, (p5, bobble) 4 times. End with p5, k1, p2, k10 (14).

Row 12: K3, lace increase, k2, yo, k2tog, k3 (7), p2, k1, p29, k1, p2, k3 (7), ssk, yo, k2, lace inc, k3 = 59 (67) sts.

Row 14: K12 (16), p2, k1, p29, k1, p2, k12 (16).

Row 16: K12 (16), p2, k1, p8, (bobble, p5) 3 times. End with p3, k1, p2, k12 (16).

Row 18: K3, lace inc, k2, yo, k2tog, k5 (9), p2, k1, p7, (bobble, p1, bobble, p3) 3 times. End with p4, k1, p2, k5 (9), ssk, yo, k2, lace inc, k3 = 63 (71) sts.

Row 20: K14 (18), p2, k1, p8, (bobble, p5) 3 times. End with p3, k1, p2, k14 (18).

Row 22: K14 (18), p2, k1, p29, k1, p2, k14 (18).

Row 24: K3, lace inc, k2, yo, k2tog, k7 (11), p2, k1, p29, k1, p2, k7 (11), ssk, yo, k2, lace inc, k3 = 67 (75) sts.

Now begin pattern repeat:

Row 26 (RS): K16 (20), p2, k1, bobbles worked as on row 6, end with k1, p2, k16 (20). Continue working in staggered bobble pattern. You'll start a new repeat on every 20th row as per row 6. The repeat = rows 6–25.

At the same time, increase at each side on every 6th row. Inc rows begin as follows: K3, lace inc, k2, yo, k2tog, bobble; work in pattern to last 7 sts, and end with ssk, yo, k2, lace inc, k3.

When piece measures approx 8¾ (9½) in / 22 (24) cm and there are a total of 99 (111) sts, work for another 8¾ in / 22 cm in pattern but without any increases at the sides. Begin pattern on row 18 (22). The lace holes should lie straight over each other (the first

and last lace holes are worked over and instead of previous lace increases).
K3, yo, k2tog, k1, yo, k2tog, etc. To mirror image on the other side, dec with ssk: the row ends with ssk, yo, k1, ssk, yo, k3.

After finishing center section, work the other side of back, reversing shaping. Wherever you increased previously, you will now decrease. Begin decreases on row 22 (16). Work the lace pattern as follows:
K3, yo, k3tog, k1, yo, k3tog; continue in pattern to last 10 sts and end row as: sssk, yo, k1, sssk, yo, k3.
Continue in pattern as set until the second sleeve matches the first one and 51 (59) sts rem. BO in pattern.

FRONT

Work as for back for the first 8¾ (9½) in / 22 (24) cm and then begin short rows on row 18 (22).
Note: do not count the yarnovers when counting sts across short rows.
Work in pattern across (omitting increases and lace holes at the sides) until 12 sts rem; turn, yo, and work back until 12 sts rem; turn, yo. Work pattern until 12 sts rem after last turn; turn, yo, work in pattern until 12 sts from last turn; turn, yo. Work in pattern until 12 sts rem from last turn;

turn, yo. Work in pattern to 12 sts from last turn. Now finish the short rows so that the yarnovers are knit through back loop with the st after yarnover. Cut yarn, leave sts on needle or on a stitch holder and work the other front the same way.

FINISHING

Steam press all the pieces under a damp towel and block then by pinning out, making sure that all measurements are correct. Sew the side and shoulder seams with mattress st.

Pick up and knit about 50 (54) sts along the straight edges on each side of back (pick up about 22 sts for every 4 in / 10 cm). Place all the picked-up and live sts from the back and front pieces on a circular US size 2.5 / 3 mm. Make sure there is an even number of stitches. Work around in k1/p1 ribbing until edging measures approx 1¾ in / 4.5 cm. BO loosely in ribbing.

With smaller short circular and RS facing, pick up and knit about 80 (100) sts along sleeve edge; join and work in stockinette for approx 1¼ in / 3 cm. BO and let edge roll forward. Finish other sleeve the same way.

1920s

The air is tense with expectation at the Theater Champs-Élysées in Paris. The audience crowds in front of the wide stage and suddenly she comes out of the darkness. A nimble woman with black glistening skin and large, rolling eyes wiggles onto the floor in a very scanty skirt of golden bananas that sways rhythmically with her provocative dance steps. Her name is Josephine Baker. The world's first black sex symbol stepped out into the footlights and quickly gained status as a muse that artists and writers, including Pablo Picasso and Luigi Pirandello, watched breathlessly when she sauntered down Paris' boulevards with her tame leopard on a leash. But even if Josephine Baker was the most celebrated idol of her time, she was not by any means the only one to move nonchalantly to the era's new sounds. The postwar world had been taken over by intoxicating pleasure seeking and the daring of the Charleston. Women were clad in straight, narrow dresses with beaded fringes that swayed in time to the music. The twenties roared with wild parties, unrestrained affairs and an implicit faith that the giddily rising stocks would soon reach the skies. But the roaring stopped suddenly. The calendar said 29 October 1929 and the world's economy went into freefall while stocks tanked on Wall Street. The party was over. From just one day to the next, darkness again descended over the dance floor and the Great Depression overtook a stunned world.

> *The postwar world has been taken over by intoxicating pleasure seeking and the daring of the Charleston. Women were clad in straight, narrow dresses with beaded fringes that swayed in time to the music*

DRESS WITH BEADED YOKE

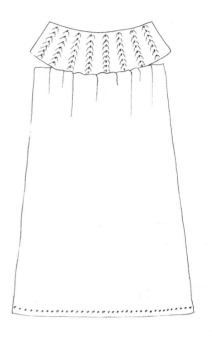

Sizes: S (M, L)

Measurements

Chest: 38½ (44, 47) in / 98 (112, 119) cm
Length below underarm: 31½ in / 80 cm

Yarn

150 (200, 200) g Wool 1, color 30 (black)
100 (150, 150) g Isager Alpaca 1, color 500
(black)

Notions: 98 (102, 108) black glass beads
about ¼ in / .5 cm diameter, beading needle
(make sure needle goes through beads easily)
and sewing thread

Needles: US sizes 4 and 8 / 3.5 and 5 mm
(16 and 32 in / 40 cm and 80 cm circulars).

Gauge

17 sts and 26 rows in lace pattern on smaller
ndls = 4 x 4 in / 10 x 10 cm.
18 sts and 26 rows in stockinette on larger
ndls with 1 strand of each yarn held together
= 4 x 4 in / 10 x 10 cm.
Adjust needle size to obtain correct gauge if
necessary.

Make 1 (m1) = 1 new st knit tbl

Lift the strand between two stitches onto
left needle and knit into back loop so that
the stitch twists. To avoid making a hole,
inc with m1.

The dress is knit in the round from the top
down. Begin with a 16 in / 40 cm circular.
Change to longer circular when stitches no
longer fit around shorter one.

DRESS

With smaller size needle and 1 strand of each yarn held together, CO 112 (119, 126) sts; join, being careful not to twist cast-on row. Work in lace pattern (multiple of 7 sts) as follows:

Rnd 1: Knit.
Rnd 2: *K1, k2tog, yo, k1, yo, ssk (or k2tog tbl), k1*; rep * to *.
Rnd 3: Knit.
Rnd 4: *K2tog, yo, k3, yo, ssk,*; rep * to *.

Repeat these 4 rnds until piece measures 1¼ in / 3 cm. Now increase 16 (17, 18) sts around:
*K1, k2tog, yo, k1, yo, ssk, k1, m1 *; rep * to *.

Continue in lace pattern, knitting the new stitches.

After 2½ in / 6 cm, increase again:
K1, k2tog, yo, k1, yo, ssk, k1, m1, k1; rep * to * = 144 (153, 162) sts.

Increase 16 (17, 18) sts the same way (*K1, k2tog, yo, k1, yo, ssk, k1, m1, k2*; rep * to *) when piece is 3½ in / 9 cm from beg = 160 (170, 180) sts. Continue in lace pattern.

When piece is 4¾ in / 12 cm, bind off for the "sleeves." Begin decreasing with a knit st at the center of a lace pattern and loosely BO a total of 32 sts (= armhole). K48 (58, 58) (= front) and BO 32 sts loosely. K48 (48, 58) (= back).

Change to larger size long circular and CO 16 (18, 20) new sts at each armhole gap. Now work in stockinette over the 128 (142, 156) sts. On the first round of the front work k1f&b into every st (front sts only, not armhole sts) so that the stitch count for the front is doubled to 96 (116, 116) sts = a total of 176 (200, 214) sts around.

Place markers around the 2 center sts at each side (before the 8th (9th, 10th) and after the 9th (10th, 11th) sts cast on for underarm) and, on every 16th rnd, m1 on each side of the marked sts (a total of 4 inc per round) = beg at left side, k1, sl marker, m1, work to first marker at right side, m1, slip marker, k2, sl marker, m1, work to last marker, m1, slip marker, k1. Work inc rnd a total of 12

times = 224 (248, 262) sts total and piece measures approx 31½ in / 80 cm from underarm. Adjust length after completing inc rnds if desired.

Finish with a lace round as follows (adjusting stitch count to a multiple of 5 by increasing or decreasing to 225 (250, 260) sts):
Yo, k3, k2tog; rep * to * around. Now work 4 garter ridges: alternately knit 1 rnd/purl 1 rnd (= 8 rnds total). BO.

Steam press the dress under a damp pressing cloth. Finish by sewing the beads to the yoke on every other stockinette st at the center of each lace pattern.

1930s

The light falls softly over her face. Her elegant silhouette moves slowly from the shadows onto the screen while the sound of rustling silk fills the air. The young actress is Greta Garbo, who, together with her colleagues Bette Davis, Katharine Hepburn and Joan Crawford, embodied the ideal woman of the time. They were products of a film industry that basked in its golden days while the world around experienced insecurity and economic chaos. These glamorous film divas smoked cigarettes, swept their wavy hair back from their faces and dressed in the latest fashions with bared shoulders, expensive jewelry and luxurious dresses tightly hugging the body's curves. Hollywood's dream factory was the big producer of female stars who, with the expert help of Parisian designers such as Coco Chanel, Elsa Schiaparelli and Madeleine Vionnet, became the idealized pictures of an unattainable life of undisturbed luxury. The contrast with reality outside the cinema's darkness is a line as sharp as the black and white photos of the film's celebrated idols, sold to faithful fans at corner newspaper stands. The world was in crisis after the stock market crash of 1929 and in America and Europe people flocked to the increasingly fantastic world of the living pictures and dreamed themselves away from joblessness, dreary housing blocks of the big cities, and looming political instability.

> These glamorous film divas smoked cigarettes, swept their wavy hair back from their faces and dressed in the latest fashions with bared shoulders, expensive jewelry and luxurious dresses tightly hugging the body's curves

DOMINO AND SHORT ROW TOP

Sizes: S/M (M/L)

Measurements

Chest: 35½ (38½) in / 90 (98) cm
Sleeve length from underarm: 17¾ (17¾) in /
45 (45) cm
Armhole depth: 8¾ (9½) in / 22 (24) cm

Yarn

Color A: 50 (50) g Viscolin, color 47 (charcoal)
Color B: 200 (300) g Viscolin, color 30 (black)
Color C: 50 (50) g Viscolin, color 36 (plum)

Needles: For top: US size 0 / 2 mm (straight
and dpn) and US 4 / 3.5 mm (straight and
long circular). For finishing, US 2.5 / 3 mm
(circular)

Gauge

32 sts and 64 rows in garter st on smaller
ndls = 4 x 4 in / 10 x 10 cm.
22 sts and 28 rows in lace pattern on large
ndls = 4 x 4 in / 10 x 10 cm.
Adjust needle size to obtain correct gauge if
necessary.

Make 1 (m1) = 1 new knit tbl st

Lift the strand between two stitches onto
left needle and knit into back loop so that
the stitch twists.

Twisted Decrease = Sl 1, k1, psso.

The yoke is knitted first.

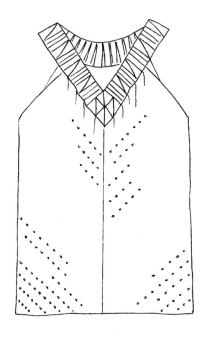

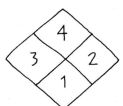

YOKE

Square 1:

With smaller ndls and color A, CO 21 sts
and work as follows:
Row 1 (WS): K10, sl 1 purlwise wyf (= relief
st), k10.
Row 2: K8, ssk, k1, k2tog, k8.
Row 3: K9, sl 1 purlwise wyf, k9.
Row 4: K7, ssk, k1, k2tog, k7.
Row 5: K8, sl 1 purlwise wyf, k8.
Row 6: K6, ssk, k1, k2tog, k6.
Row 7: K7, sl 1 purlwise wyf, k7.
Row 8: K5, ssk, k1, k2tog, k5.
Row 9: K6, sl 1 purlwise wyf, k6.
Row 10: K4, ssk, k1, k2tog, k4.
Row 11: K5, sl 1 purlwise wyf, k5.
Row 12: K3, ssk, k1, k2tog, k3.
Row 13: K4, sl 1 purlwise wyf, k4.
Row 14: K2, ssk, k1, k2tog, k2.
Row 15: K3, sl 1 purlwise wyf, k3.
Row 16: K1, ssk, k1, k2tog, k1.
Row 17: K2, sl 1 purlwise wyf, k2.
Row 18: Ssk, k1, k2tog.

Row 19: K1, sl 1 purlwise wyf, k1.
Row 20: K1-k2tog-psso.
Cut yarn and pull yarn through rem st but
do not tighten.

Square 2:

With smaller ndls and color B, CO 10 sts
and then, with RS of square 1 facing, pick
up and knit 10 sts through "knots" along the
upper right side of square 1 and then pick
up and knit 1 st at tip of square 1 = 21 sts.
Work as for rows 1–20 of square 1.

Square 3:

With smaller ndls and color B, pick up and
knit 11 sts along the knot edge on the left
side of square 1 and then CO 10 sts. Work
rows 1–20 as for square 1 over these 21 sts.

Square 4:

With color C, pick up and knit 21 sts between squares 2 and 3 as follows: pick up
and knit 10 sts along the knot edge on the
left side of square 2, 1 st at tip between

squares 2 and 3, and 10 sts along knot edge of square 3. Work rows 1–20 as for square 1 over these 21 sts.

Now, with smaller ndls and color A, pick and knit 20 sts along top right edge of squares 2 and 4 and work a ridge row:
Row 1 (WS, top edge): Sl 1 purlwise, sl 1 purlwise wyf (relief st), k16, sl 1 purlwise wyf, k1.
Row 2: K20.
Repeat rows 1 and 2 until there are a total of 4 ridges (= 8 rows).
Change to color B and rep rows 1 and 2 for a total of 2 ridges (= 4 rows).
Note: For smooth color changes, knit with new and old colors into the last st of the WS rows.
Change to color C and knit 4 ridges; ending with a WS row.

Change to color B and make Gusset 1 with short rows:
Row 1 (RS): Knit.
Row 2: Sl 1 purlwise, sl 1 purlwise wyf, k13, turn.
Row 3: Yo, k15.
Row 4: Sl 1 purlwise, sl 1 purlwise wyf, k8, turn.
Row 5: Yo, k10.
Row 6: Sl 1 purlwise, sl 1 purlwise wyf, k3, turn.
Row 7: Yo, k5.
Row 8: Sl 1 purlwise, sl 1 purlwise wyf, k3, 2tog tbl with yo and next st, k4, k2tog tbl with yo and next st, k4, k2tog tog with yo and next st, k2, sl 1 purlwise, k1.

Change to color A and work Gusset 2:
Row 1 (RS): Knit.
Row 2: Sl 1 purlwise, sl 1 purlwise wyf, k16, sl 1 purlwise wyf, k1.
Row 3: K15, turn.
Row 4: Yo, k13, sl 1 purlwise wyf, k1.
Row 5: K10, turn.
Row 6: Yo, k8, sl 1 purlwise wyf, k1.
Row 7: K5, turn.

Row 8: Yo, k3, sl 1 purlwise wyf, k1.
Row 9: K5, (k2tog with yo and next st, k4) 3 times.
Row 10: Sl 1 purlwise, sl 1 purlwise wyf, k16, sl 1 purlwise wyf, k1.
Change to color B and knit 3 ridges (= 6 rows).
Change to color C and knit 2 ridges (= 4 rows).
Change to color A and knit 3 ridges.
Change to color B and knit Gusset 1.
Change to color C and knit Gusset 2. On size S/M: Sl 1 purlwise at beg of every row. The knot edge stops at this point so that later you can pick up and knit sts from this edge. On size M/L continue as before.
Change to color B and knit 2 ridges. (*Note:* on sizes M/L, sl 1 purlwise beg of every row). Don't forget that the 1st st on all rows is slipped purlwise.
With A, knit 4 ridges.
With B, knit 2 ridges.
With C, knit 4 ridges.
With A, knit Gusset 2.
With B, knit Gusset 1.
With C, knit 2 ridges.
With A, knit 4 ridges.

With B, knit Gusset 3 as follows:
Row 1: Sl 1 purlwise, k13, turn.
Row 2: Yo, k12, sl 1 purlwise wyf, k1.
Row 3: Sl 1 purlwise, k6, turn.
Row 4: Yo, k5, sl 1 purlwise wyf, k1.
Row 5: Sl 1 purlwise, k6, k2tog with yo and next st, k6, k2tog with yo and next st, k5.
Row 6: Sl 1 purlwise, sl 1 purlwise wyf, k16, sl 1 purlwise wyf, k1.

With A, knit 5 ridges.
With C, knit Gusset 3.
With B, knit 5 ridges.
With C, knit Gusset 3.
With A, knit 5 ridges.
With B, knit Gusset 3.
With C, knit 5 ridges, so that the 1st st on size S/M on the lowest edge from now on is knitted (= knot edge) – sts for the back will be picked up from here. Size M/L: continue as set.

(Size M/L only: Change to color B and knit 3 ridges, knitting the 1st st at lowest edge from now on.)

Both sizes:
With A, knit Gusset 3.
With B, knit 5 ridges.
With A, knit Gusset 3.
With C, knit 5 ridges.
With B, knit Gusset 3.
With A, knit 5 ridges.
(Size M/L only: change to color C and knit 5 ridges.)

Both sizes: With B, knit Gusset 3.

Place sts on a holder and work the other side of yoke. The gussets are worked slightly differently on this side of yoke:
Gusset 1: Begin on row 2, work rows 3-8, and then row 1. On row 8, note that the yarnover is knit together with the st following it. Make sure that the edges sts are worked correctly.
Gusset 2: Begin with row 2, work rows 3-10, and then work row 1. On row 9, ssk the yarnover with st following it.
Gusset 3: Begin with row 6 and then work rows 1-5. On row 5, ssk the yarnover with the st following it.

On size S/M, work 5 ridges with A (on size M/L, knit 5 ridges with C), before ending with B. The right side finishes with Gusset 3 in black and is at the center back. With RS facing RS and using a 3rd dpn, knit the 2 sides together with three-needle bind-off. Weave in all tails on WS.

Front

With B and smaller ndls, pick up and knit 89 (97) sts along knot edge of front. Change to larger ndls and begin on WS:
Row 1: Sl 1 purlwise, p1, k1f&b into each of next 42 (46) sts, p1, k1f&b into each of next 42 (46) sts, p1, k1 = 173 (189) sts total.
Row 2 (RS): Sl 1 purlwise, k2tog, k83 (91),

m1, k1 (= center st), m1, k83 (91), ssk, k1.
Row 3 (WS): Sl 1 purlwise, p171 (187), k1.

Repeat rows 2 and 3 once and then work lace pattern on row 6:
Row 6: Sl 1 purlwise, k2tog, *k2tog, yo*; rep * to * 41 (45) times (to the center st), m1, k1, m1, *yo, ssk*; rep * to * until 3 sts rem and end ssk, k1.

Continue in pattern, repeating rows 2 and 3 (beg with row 3 on WS) and working lace pattern on every 6th row. Count sts occasionally to make sure the stitch count is consistent.
When front is 4¾ (5½) in / 12 (14) cm long (not including yoke), set front aside and work back.

Back

With B and smaller ndls, pick up and knit 64 (72) sts along knot edge of back. Change to larger ndls.
Next row is WS: Sl 1 purlwise, and then k1f&b into every other st = 95 (107) sts total.
Pattern repeat for back is: work 5 rows in stockinette (always beginning every row with sl 1 purlwise) and then work 6th row in lace pattern as for front.

After working pattern for 6¼ (7) in / 16 (18) cm, ending with the same number of rows from the last lace row on both back and front, place all sts on larger circular. Now work around in stockinette and lace pattern and, *at the same time*, on front, continue increasing on every other rnd at the center st and decreasing at each side.
Continue working around in pattern until piece measures 15 in / 38 cm or desired length, as measured from "the point" of the front. BO center st and then work back and forth in lace pattern on front only. On every other row, k2tog at beg of row and ssk at end of row on each side of the front point so that the lower edge will be straight. Don't forget to decrease at the sides.

When all the front sts have been eliminated, with a smaller needle (US size 2.5 / 3 mm), pick up and knit about 22 sts per 4 in / 10 cm evenly spaced along the front edge and knit around in stockinette on back and front sts for approx ¾ in / 2 cm and then BO.

FINISHING

Fold the facing around lower edge to WS so that it hides the edge of picked-up stitches and sew down with small stitches.

Weave in all ends neatly on WS and steam press the top under a damp pressing cloth.

1940s

While the boulevards of Paris are dark, the One Two Two nightclub is lit up. The popular singer Edith Piaf is performing and, despite her tiny figure, the whole room fills with her double entendre songs about love and freedom before an audience of high ranking Nazi officers. Her boyfriend is the young Jewish composer and womanizer, Norbert Glanzberg, so she is living a dangerous life. The year is 1941, the world is at war, and, with the Nazi deportations of Jews, gypsies, and intellectuals, darkness has fallen over Europe. Adolf Hitler is saluted by enthusiastic crowds of people in Berlin and it has been decided by law that Jews must wear the yellow Star of David with "Jew" inscribed on it on the left side of the chest. At another place in Europe — in Kz-lejre Auschwitz — a new type of building is going on: in a deviously-arranged extermination center, the first gruesome experiments with mass killing are underway. The vents open and the deadly poisonous gas Zyklon B is released, killing 850 Polish and Soviet prisoners of war. The deaths took place in a specially designed industrial complex with just one goal in mind. By the time the war is over, 6 million Jews have been massacred. Among the survivors is Norbert Glanzberg, who was able to leave Paris with Edith Piaf's help before the first trains left in the direction of the death camps at Treblinka, Belzec and Sobibór.

> The year is 1941, the world is at war, and with the Nazi deportations of Jews, gypsies, and intellectuals, darkness has fallen over Europe

GIRL'S CARDIGAN

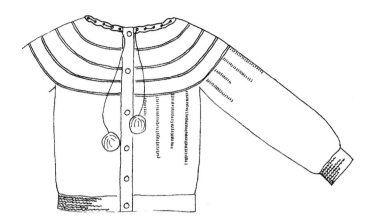

Sizes: 3–4 years (7–8 years)

Measurements
Chest: 26½ (28¼) in / 67 (72) cm
Length below underarm: 9¾ (11¾) in / 25 (30) cm
Sleeve length: 11 (14¼) in / 28 (36) cm
Sleeve width at cuff: 6 (6¾) in /15 (17) cm
Sleeve width: 9 (10¼) in / 23 (26) cm
Length at yoke: 5¼ (6) in / 13 (15) cm

Yarn
Color A: worked with 1 strand of each yarn held together.
100 (100) g Isager Wool 1, color 28s (red)
100 (100) g Tvinni, color 28s (coral on gray)

Color B: worked with 2 strands held together.
50 g Tvinni, color 46s (mint)

Color C: worked with 2 strands held together.
50 g Tvinni, color 37 (bottle green)

Notions: 6 mint-colored buttons about ½ in / 1.3 cm diameter; for smaller size only: silk ribbon just long enough to tie into a bow through neck casing.

Needles: US size 6 / 4 mm (24 or 32 in / 60 or 80 cm circular).

Gauge
20 sts and 48 rows in garter st with 2 strands held together = 4 x 4 in / 10 x 10 cm.
19 sts and 32 rows in column pattern with 2 strands held together = 4 x 4 in / 10 x 10 cm.
20 sts and 34 rows in 3-color pattern with 2 strands held together = 4 x 4 in / 10 x 10 cm.
Adjust needle size to obtain correct gauge if necessary.

The cardigan is worked back and forth on a circular, beginning at lower edge. The back and front are knitted as one piece. *Don't forget that each of the colors is worked with 2 strands of yarn held together.*

Note: all slip sts are slipped purlwise (insert ndl into st as if to purl but do not work, simply slide st to right ndl).

Back and Front

With A, CO 116 (128) sts and work garter st edge as follows:

Row 1 (WS): K1, sl 1 purlwise wyf (= relief st), k112 (124), sl 1 wyf, k1.

Row 2: Knit.

Repeat these 2 rows until edge measures 1½ (2) in / 4 (5) cm. On the last row (WS), increase 8 (6) sts evenly spaced across (do not increase on edge sts) to 124 (134) sts as follows:

For smaller size: K1, sl 1 purlwise wyf, k7, (m1, k14) 7 times, m1, k7, sl 1 wyf, k1.

For larger size: K1, sl 1 purlwise wyf, k12, (m1, k20) 5 times, m1, k12, sl 1 wyf, k1.

Now continue in Column pattern as follows:

Row 1 (RS): K2, p2 (4), *sl 2 wyf (= 2 relief sts), p4*. Rep * to * until 6 (8) sts rem and end with sl 2 wyf, p2 (4), k2.

Row 2: K1, sl 1 wyf, k2 (4), *p2, k4*. Rep * to * until 6 (8) sts rem and end with p2, k2 (4), sl 1 wyf, k1.

Repeat rows 1 and 2 of column pattern until piece measures 9¾ (11¾) in / 25 (30) cm from cast-on edge.

BO for underarm on RS:

Work 26 (27) sts in pattern, BO 6 (8) sts, 60 (64) sts in pattern, BO 6 (8), 26 (27) pattern sts. Set piece aside.

Sleeves (worked back and forth)

With A, CO 30 (34) sts and work garter st cuff:

Row 1 (WS): K1, sl 1 wyf, k26 (30), sl 1 wyf, k1.

Row 2: Knit across.

Rep these 2 rows until cuff measures 1½ (2) in / 4 (5) cm and, on the last row (WS), inc evenly spaced across (do not increase on edge sts) to 44 (50) sts as follows:

For smaller size: K1, sl 1 wyf, m1, (k2, m1) 13 times, sl 1 wyf, k1.

For larger size: K1, sl 1 wyf, m1 (k2, m1) 15 times, sl 1 wyf, k1.

Now work in Column pattern:

Row 1 (RS): K2, *p4, sl 2 wyf*. Rep * to * until 6 (6) sts rem and end with p4, k2.

Row 2: K1, sl 1 wyf, *k4, p2*; Rep * to * until 6 (6) sts rem and end with k4, sl 1 wyf, k1.

Rep these 2 rows until sleeve measures 11 (14¼) in / 28 (36) cm from cast-on row.

Now shape underarm by binding off 4 (5) sts at beg of next 2 rows (the first and last sts bound-off will be used later for seaming) = 36 (40) sts rem. Set sleeve aside and work the other sleeve the same way.

Yoke

Place pieces on long circular: 26 (27) sts of left front, 1 sleeve, 36 (40) sts, back 60 (64) sts, sleeve 36 (40) sts, right front 26 (27). With A, work back on WS in pattern over all 184 (198) sts, increasing 1 st (for example on back) for a total of 185 (199) sts.

Now begin working back and forth in the three-color pattern and, *at the same time,* decrease around the yoke for neck shaping as follows:

For size 3–4 years, begin on row 9 (for size 7–8 years, beg on row 1).

Row 1 (RS), with B (2 strands held together): Knit across.

Row 2: K1, sl 1 wyf, k181 (195), sl 1 wyf, k1.

Row 3, with C (2 strands held together): K3, *sl 1 wyb, k1*; Rep * to * and end with k2.

Row 4: K1, sl 1 wyf, k1, *sl 1 with wyf, k1*. Rep * to * and end with sl 1 wyf, k1.

Rows 5 and 6 (with B): As for rows 1–2.

Row 7, with A (one strand of each yarn held together): K2, *sl 1 wyb, k1*. Rep * to * and end with k1.

Row 8: K1, sl 1 wyf, *sl 1 wyf, p1*. Rep * to * and end with sl 2 wyf, k1.

Row 9: Knit across.

Row 10: K1, sl 1 wyf, p181 (195), sl 1 wyf, k1.

Row 11: Knit across.

Row 12: K1, sl 1 wyf, p181 (195), sl 1 wyf, k1.

Repeat these 12 rows 3 (3) times, but, *at the same time,* on every 11th pattern row (a total of 3 dec rows) dec 30, 38, 46 (36, 40, 48) sts evenly spaced across with k2tog. After the final decrease row, 71 (75) sts rem.

End with a lace row with color B.

Row 1 (RS): Knit across.

Row 2: K1, sl 1 wyf, k67 (71), sl 1 wyf, k1.

Row 3: K2, *k2tog, yo*; rep * to * and end with k3.

Note: Make sure that stitch count stays consistent when working lace.

Row 4: As for row 2.

Change to color A and work rows 1 and 2 and then BO.

Lightly steam press cardigan under a damp pressing cloth and join sleeve seams and underarms with mattress st.

Left Front band: With A, pick up and knit 70 (80) sts along knot edge of left front and then knit 10 rows, always slipping the 1st of each row purlwise to create a chain edge. BO.

Right Front band: Work as for left front band, making buttonholes on rows 5–6:

Row 5 (RS): K4, *BO 2, k10 (12)*; rep * to * and end with k4 [instead of k10 (12)].

Row 6: K4, *CO 2 new sts over gap, k10 (12)*; rep * to * and end with k4 [instead of k10 (12)].

Note: number of sts to knit after buttonhole BO include the st left over from BO.

Knit the final 4 rows of band and BO.

FINISHING

Size 7–8 years

Twist a cord about 59 in / 150 cm long as follows:

With C, cut 6 strands, each about 138 in (about 3.8 yds) / 350 cm long. Tie one end of the strands around a door knob and knot the other end. Insert a pencil or something similar into the knot and then twist the cord, holding the yarn with the other hand. When the cord is twisted so much that it starts to twist back on itself, hold it straight out from the door knob, grab it at the center and fold it in half, letting it twist evenly; smooth out cord as necessary. Knot each end and thread cord through lace row at neck.

Pompom: Cut out 2 small circles about 1¾–2 in / 4 or 5 cm diameter and then cut out a hole 3/8–3/4 in / 1–2 cm diameter at the center. Holding the templates together and 2 strands of color C, wrap yarn through the template until the hole is completely filled. Cut the yarn along the outermost edge by inserting the scissors between the 2 pieces of paper.

Tightly wind a heavy thread between the paper circles and tie a solid knot. Cut a slit into the template to remove it. Carefully steam and trim the pompom.

Make one more pompom the same way and secure one to each end of cord.

Sew buttons onto cardigan.

Note: For the smaller size I recommend using a silk ribbon instead of the cord with pompoms. Cut the ribbon just long enough to tie into a bow; otherwise it could be dangerous for small children.

BRIOCHE STITCH CARDIGAN

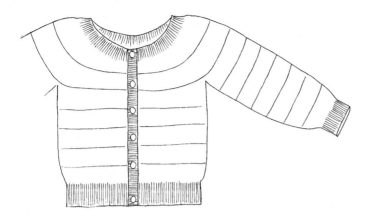

Sizes: S (M, L)

Measurements

Chest: 34 (35, 36¼) in / 86 (89, 92) cm
Body length below underarm: 14¼ (14¼, 15) in / 36 (36, 38) cm
Sleeve length from underarm: 17¾ (18½, 20) in / 45 (47, 51) cm

Yarn

400 (450, 500) g Tvinni, color 37 (bottle green). 2 strands of yarn are held together for brioche pattern.

Notions: 6 (6, 6) red buttons, 5/8 in / 1.5 cm diameter

Needles: US size 6 / 4 mm (24 and 32 in / 60 and 80 cm circulars).

Gauge

18 sts and 44 rows in brioche st (2 strands held together) = 4 x 4 in / 10 x 10 cm.
24 sts and 28 rows in k1/p1 ribbing (2 strands held together) = 4 x 4 in / 10 x 10 cm.
Adjust needle size to obtain correct gauge if necessary.

Double Decrease

Slip 1 st, k2tog (a knit and a purl st tog), pass the slipped st over.

The cardigan is worked back and forth, beginning at lower edge. Back and front are worked in one piece. Yarn is doubled for brioche pattern and single for ribbing between brioche sections. Carry unused strand up side.

BACK AND FRONT

With 2 strands of yarn held together, CO
173 (183, 193) sts and work back and forth
in ribbing as follows:

Ribbing

Row 1 (WS): K1, *p1, k1*; rep * to * across.

Row 2: K1, *k1, p1*; rep * to * and end with k2.

Repeat rows 1 and 2 until ribbing measures
approx 3¼ in / 8 cm. On the last RS row,
decrease to 147 (153, 159) sts evenly spaced
across with double decrease (described
above) 13 (15, 17) times across.

Now begin brioche pattern:

Row 1 (WS): K1, *yo, sl 1 purlwise wyb,
k1*. Rep * to *.

Row 2: K1, *k2tog, yo, sl 1 purlwise wyb*; rep
* to * until 3 sts rem and end with k2tog, k1.

Row 3: K1, *yo, sl 1 purlwise wyb, k2tog*;
rep * to * until 2 sts rem and end with yo, sl
1 purlwise wyb, k1.

Rep rows 2 and 3 until you've worked a total
of 20 (22, 24) rows (= 1 brioche section) and
the brioche knitting = 1½ (2, 2¼) in / 4.5 (5,
5.5) cm.

With only 1 strand of yarn, work in ribbing
as follows:

Row 1: K1, *k2tog, p1*; rep * to * and end
with k2tog, k1.

Row 2: *K1, p1*; rep * to * and end with k1.

Now, with 2 strands of yarn held together,
work in brioche pattern for 20 (22, 24) rows
and then work the 2 rows of ribbing pattern.

Repeat the pattern sequence of brioche and
ribbing until piece measures 14¼ (14¼, 15)
in / 36 (36, 38) cm from cast-on row and
you've worked 4 rep of single strand ribbing

+ 19 (21, 23) rows of brioche (2 strands of
yarn).

On the next row, bind off for underarms:
Work 32 (34, 36) sts brioche, loosely BO 7 sts,
69 (71, 73) sts brioche, loosely BO 7 sts, 32
(34, 36) sts brioche. *Note:* number of sts to knit
after BO include the st left over from BO).
 Set piece aside while you knit sleeves.

SLEEVES

With 2 strands of yarn held together, CO
41 (45, 49) sts and work back and forth in
ribbing:

Row 1 (WS): K1, *p1, k1*; rep * to * across.

Row 2: K1, *k1, p1*; rep * to * to last 2 sts
and end with k2.

Rep these 2 rows until cuff measures 2 (1½,
1½) in / 5 (4, 4) cm.

Note: if you want shorter sleeves, work fewer
rows on the cuffs.

On last row of ribbing (WS), work double
increase 6 times evenly spaced across:
Lift strand between 2 sts onto left needle
and k1f&b into loop = 2 new sts. This increase
does not make a hole in the knit fabric.
There should now be 53 (57, 61) sts.

Continue in brioche (20 (22, 24) rows) and
rib (2 rows) patterns as for body. Don't forget
that the brioche is worked with 2 strands
and the ribbing with 1.

At the same time, after the 3rd brioche panel,
inc with double increase 3 times across the
2nd row of ribbing = 59 (63, 67) sts.

Rep the double increase (3 times across) on
the 2nd ribbing row after another 3 brioche
panels (= 6 brioche panels total) = 65 (69,
73) sts.

When you've worked 18 (20, 22) rows of the
8th brioche panel and sleeve measures approx
17¾ (18½, 20) in / 45 (47, 51) cm from cast-on,
shape underarm. BO 4 sts at beg of next two

rows. In order for the pieces to fit together well, the underarm shaping is on the last 2 rows before the ribbing for the sleeves but on the last row before the ribbing on the back/front.

YOKE

Place all sts on a long circular: 32 (34, 36) sts of right front, right sleeve, 57 (61, 65) sts, back 69 (71, 73) sts, left sleeve 57 (61, 65) sts, and left front 32 (34, 36) sts = 247 (261, 275) sts total.

The first row is a RS ribbing row and beg of yoke shaping:
Dec 40 (42, 44) sts evenly spaced across making 20 (21, 22) double decreases as follows: Rib 7 (9, 11) sts, (dbl dec, rib 9) 20 (21, 22) times = 207 (219, 231) sts rem. Work WS ribbing row and the brioche panel.
On next RS ribbing row, dec 40 (42, 44) sts with double decreases evenly spaced across (dec above decreases of previous dec row) = 167 (177, 187) sts rem.

After working the 10th (12th, 14th) brioche row of the 3rd panel on the yoke, begin short rows to shape neck.

Continuing in brioche pattern, work across until 6 sts rem; turn, yo and work back until 6 sts rem on other side; turn, yo and work back until 12 sts (do not include yarnovers in stitch count) rem; turn, yo and work back until 12 sts rem, yo; turn. Continue, with 6 fewer sts worked each time until 24 sts remain at each side. Now work across all sts, knitting the yarnovers together with the following stitch through back loops.

On the next row, work in ribbing with *2 strands. At the same time,* dec 18 (20, 22) sts evenly spaced around neck with 9 (10, 11) double decreases:
Size S: Rib 17 (dbl dec, rib 15) 8 times, dbl dec, rib 3.
Size M: Rib 17 (dbl dec, rib 14) 9 times, dbl dec, rib 4.
Size L: Rib 12 (dbl dec, rib 14) 10 times, dbl dec, rib 2.
 = 149 (157, 165) sts rem.
Continue in ribbing and, on the 6th row dec 18 (20, 22) sts evenly spaced across (dec above and centered between each previous dec) = 131 (137, 143) sts rem.
On the 12th row, dec 21 (23, 25) sts evenly spaced (about every 6th (6th, 5th) st) around neck and, *at the same time,* BO knitwise.

FINISHING

Seam sleeves with mattress stitch.

Left front band: With 2 strands held together, pick up and knit 89 (95, 101) sts along knot edge of left front. Work 7 rows in k1/p1 ribbing, always slipping the 1st st of each row purlwise. BO knitwise on row 8.
Right front band: Work as for left front band, but, on row 4, make 6 (6, 6) buttonholes: Work 6 (4, 5) sts, (BO 2, rib 13 (15, 16) sts), 4 (5, 5) times and end with BO 2 and rib 6 (4, 4) sts. On the next row, CO 2 sts over each gap. Continue in ribbing and BO knitwise on row 8.

Sew on buttons spaced as for buttonholes.

1950s

The jerkily twisting hips reverberated through a wave of screaming girls. With a quick grab of the microphone, he pointed self-assuredly at the public while his lips curled to the side of an impertinent smile. It was June 5, 1956, the TV studio was boiling hot, and the king had arrived! His name was Elvis Aaron Presley but the recording studio and his new manager quickly transformed the young truck driver, who had grown up poor in Memphis, Tennessee into a charismatic teen idol. The world had never seen anything like it before. Now his name was just Elvis. From coast to coast, more than 40 million Americans watched on TV to see his performances—and the day after all hell broke loose. Newspaper columns seethed with rage and self-appointed moralists warned about youth going to ruin, ministers preached against his daring body language, and the white middle class condemned the inspiration from black gospel and blues. In the meantime, their sons and daughters were consumed by "You ain't nothin' but a hound dog." They pomaded their hair and dreamed sweet dreams about fleeing the suburbs behind the wheel of a Cadillac with a Confederate flag decal and themselves dressed in tight-fitting leather jackets. Elvis gave youth a new ideal when he used his body and voice to express his generation's rebellion against bourgeois conformity. A new genre was born—rock'n'roll.

> From coast to coast, more than 40 million Americans watched on TV to see his performances—and the day after all hell broke loose

Cape

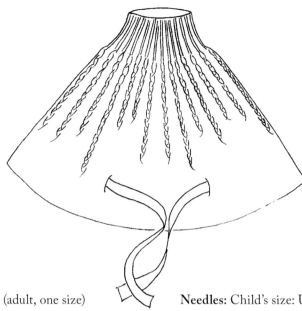

Sizes: 5–6 years (adult, one size)

The cape is designed for child and adult sizes. The size depends on the type of yarn and size of needles used; the stitch count is the same for both sizes.

Measurements

Child size 5–6 years:
Neck circumference: approx 15 in / 38 cm.
Circumference at shoulders: approx 34 in / 86 cm.
Circumference at lower edge: 56¾ in / 144 cm
Length from 1st increase: approx 13½ in / 34 cm.
Length from 1st increase to waist: 9½ in / 24 cm.

Adult:
Neck circumference: 22¾ in / 58 cm.
Circumference at shoulders: 48 in / 122 cm.
Circumference at lower edge: 80 in / 202 cm.
Length from 1st increase: 19 in / 48 cm.
Length from 1st increase to waist: 13¾ in / 35 cm.

Yarn

Child's size: 150 g Isager Alpaca 2, color 021 (light chartreuse)
Adult: 600 g Isager Alpaca 2 color 2105 (natural gray)

Needles: Child's size: US size 2.5 / 3 mm; Adult: US size 7 / 4.5 mm (short and long circulars).

Gauge

24 sts and 38 rows in cable pattern with 1 strand Isager Alpaca 2 on smaller ndls (child size) = 4 x 4 in / 10 x 10 cm.
28 sts and 40 rows in k2/p2 ribbing (slightly stretched) with 1 strand Isager Alpaca 2 on smaller ndls (child) = 4 x 4 in / 10 x 10 cm.

17 sts and 24 rows in cable pattern with 2 strands Isager Alpaca 2 on larger ndls (adult) = 4 x 4 in / 10 x 10 cm.
18 sts and 26 rows in k2/p2 ribbing (slightly stretched) with 2 strands Isager Alpaca 2 on larger ndls (adult) = 4 x 4 in / 10 x 10 cm.

Adjust needle size to obtain correct gauge if necessary.

The cape is knit in the round from the top down. The child's size uses 1 strand of yarn and the adult 2 strands held together throughout.

CAPE

With short circular and yarn/ndls for chosen size, CO 104 sts; join, being careful not to twist cast-on row. Work in p2/k2 ribbing until neck measures approx 2¾ (4¾) in / 7 (12) cm.

Now inc with m1 on each side of the knit ribs (lift strand between 2 sts and knit into back loop; this inc avoids a hole) = 156 sts and 4 purl ribs between each knit rib. When stitches no longer fit around short circular, switch to longer ndl.

Now work in cable pattern:

Rnd 1:*P4. Join the next 2 sts by inserting needle through both and making 5 sts as follows: k1, p1, k1, p1, k1*. Rep * to *.

Rnd 2: Work knit over knit and purl over purl; knit the new sts.

Rnd 3: *P4, k3, k2tog*; rep * to *.

Rnds 4, 6, and 8: Work knit over knit and purl over purl.

Rnd 5: *P4, k2, k2tog*; rep * to * around.

Rnd 7: *P4, k1, k2tog*; rep * to * around.

Rnd 9: *P4, k2*; rep * to * around.

Rnd 10: Work knit over knit and purl over purl.

Repeat these 10 rnds. After 15 rnds, inc 52 sts around with m1 on each side of every bobble column. *The new sts are always purled.* Rep the increase rnd on every 25th rnd, 2 times.

When piece measures approx 9½ in / 24 cm (approx 13¾ in / 35 cm, from the first inc rnd, make the "loops" for the belt:

Place a safety pin into the center loop of the purl sts between 2 columns, work across 4 columns and then pm in the center loop between the 4th and 5th columns, work across 9 columns and pm between the 9th

and 10th columns, work over 4 columns and pm between the 4th and 5th columns. You've now marked the 4 stitches where the belt "loops" will be placed. Working each section separately, work 10 (8) rows back and forth in pattern on each section; the outermost st on each side of the columns is slipped purlwise to form a chain edge. The sts on each side of the column are knitted on both RS and WS rows.

At the same time, after you've worked the 25th row following the last inc, inc again but this time, inc on each side of the columns of the "sleeve" sts. Do not inc at the sides of the columns in the 5 previous and the 5 backmost areas which are the "front" and "back."

When the "belt loops" have been finished, place all the sts on a needle and continue in pattern as before. Work for about 2½ in / 6 cm, or to desired length, without increasing and then BO, being careful not to bind off too tightly.

BELT
The belt is worked in double knitting on smaller (larger) ndls as follows:
CO 14 sts with 1 strand (2 strands) Alpaca 2.
Row 1: Sl 1 purlwise, *k1, sl 1 purlwise wyf*; rep * to * and end with k1. Repeat this row until belt measures about 55¼ in / 140 cm (approx 63 in /160 cm). Finish by first knitting 2 tog across and then BO.

Weave in all yarn tails neatly on WS and then steam press cape lightly under a damp pressing cloth. Thread belt through openings.

1960s

"In the future, everyone will be world famous for 15 minutes." The year is 1968 and the words are Andy Warhol's. In a run-down apartment block in New York's midtown Manhattan a young artist settled down in a loft studio surrounded by his works—gigantic silk prints of the Hollywood icon Marilyn Monroe in an explosion of bright colors, pictures of Coca-Cola bottles and cans of Campbell's Tomato Soup, as well as countless rolls of film taken with a hand-held camera of his eccentric friends from the city's artistic underground. The place was known as the Factory. While the most forward thinking reviewers wrote enthusiastically about a totally new era in American art,

> "In the future, everyone will be world famous for 15 minutes." The year is 1968 and the words are Andy Warhol's.

New York's bourgeoisie was scandalized by Warhol's outrageous parties where the guests drowned themselves and each other in a cocktail of champagne and amphetamines, orgies of sexual excesses, and political happenings. The popular actress Edie Sedgewick, graffiti artist Jean-Michel Basquiat, and the decadent journalist Truman Capote, as well as the musicians in the Velvet Underground were always invited—and, long after the lights were extinguished and the last guest left The Factory, Andy Warhol is still an icon for his time with a fame that will last much longer than the predicted 15 minutes.

Two-Color Brioche Sweater and Cap

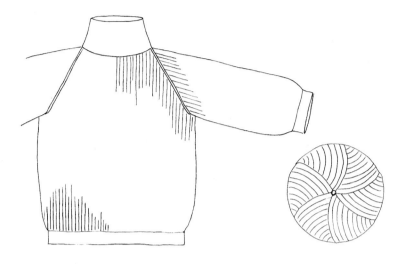

Sizes: S/M (M/L)
Cap: one size

Measurements

Sweater:
Chest: 35½ (39½) in / 90 (100) cm
Sleeve length from neckline: 19¾ (20½) in / 50 (52) cm.
Total length: 21¾ (23¼) in / 55 (59) cm.

Cap: Circumference at lower edge: 19 in / 48 cm.

Yarn

Sweater:
250 (300) g Isager Alpaca 2, color 500 (black)
200 (250) g Tvinni, color 0 (white)
If you want to knit the cap in addition to the sweater, you'll need 50 g more Isager 2, color 500 (black).

Needles: US size 7 / 4.5 mm (16 in / 40 cm and 24 or 32 in / 60 or 80 cm circular for sweater and 16 in / 40 cm circular for cap).

Gauge

24 sts and 32 rows in k1/p1 ribbing and 2 strands held together = 4 x 4 in / 10 x 10 cm. 16 sts and 40 rows in two-color brioche and 2 strands held together = 4 x 4 in / 10 x 10 cm. Adjust needle size to obtain correct gauge if necessary.

Double decrease (sl 1 – k2tog – psso)

Sl 1 knitwise, k2tog, and pass slipped st over.

Two-color brioche

Make a swatch first so that you can learn how to do the pattern and to make sure that your gauge is correct. If the gauge is not right, try again with smaller or larger needles.

GAUGE SWATCH

With circular or a dpn, CO 17 sts with 2 strands of black held together and begin on RS and work set-up row (mark RS with a contrast color thread or locking stitch marker):
K1, *k1, p1*; rep * to * until 2 sts rem and end with k2.

Notes:
1. To purl into purl below: bring yarn to front, insert ndl from right to left down into purl ridge, yarn around ndl and through ridge to complete purl st; slip st on left ndl off.
2. To knit into knit below: with yarn in back, insert ndl into center of knit st, yarn around ndl and through st to complete knit; slip st on left ndl off.
3. The color of the stitch below that you are working into should be the same color as the one you are working across row with.
4. When both yarns are at the same side, bring color to be used next up in front of old color.

Now begin 4-row two-color brioche pattern. Slide the sts back to end of needle and begin the next row from the same side as set-up row (RS).
Change to 2 strands of white held together and work in two-color brioche as follows:

Row 1 (RS with white): K1, *k1, p1 into stitch below*. Rep * to * until 2 sts rem and end with k2. Turn.
Row 2 (WS with black): K1, *p1 into stitch below, k1*. Rep * to * until 2 sts rem and end with p1 into st below, k1. Slide sts to front of ndl.
Row 3 (WS, with white): K1, *p1, k1 into st below*. Rep * to * until 2 sts rem and end with p1, k1. Turn.
Row 4 (RS with black): K1, *k1 into st below, p1*. Rep * to * until 2 sts rem and end with k1 into st below, k1. Slide sts to front of ndl.

Rep these 4 rows and then BO when swatch measures about 4 in / 10 cm.

SWEATER

The sweater is worked back and forth on a long circular, beginning at lower edge. It is finished by sewing the side and raglan seams. The first and last sts of each row are always knitted.

BACK

With 2 strands of black Isager Alpaca 2 held together and long circular, CO 89 (97) sts and work in ribbing:
Row 1 (WS): K1, *p1, k1*; rep * to *.
Row 2: K1, *k1, p1*; rep * to * and end with k2.
Rep these 2 rows until ribbing measures 1½ in / 4 cm. On the last RS row, dec to 71 (79) sts evenly spaced across by working the double dec described above 9 times so that the pattern will continue.

Add white Tvinni and continue in two-color brioche as for the gauge swatch until piece measures approx 14¼ (15) in / 36 (38) cm from cast-on row. At beg of the 3rd and 4th pattern rows, BO 4 sts each = 63 (71) sts rem.

Now dec for raglan shaping (on a row 1) with a double dec inside the edge st at each side. Don't forget that the outermost st at each side throughout is knitted so that you'll have an edge for seaming. Work the first dec as follows:
K1, k3tog, 55 (63) sts brioche, sl 1-ssk-psso, k1. Work decreases the same way on every 12th row with the double dec at each side a total of 4 times (including 1st dec) and then on every 8th row with dbl dec at each side 4 (5) times. You've now decreased 16 (18) sts at each side and the piece measures approx 8 (8¾) in / 20 (22) cm from the underarm. Place rem 31 (35) sts on a holder.

FRONT

Work as for back and BO loosely.
To shape neckline, measure down 1¾ in / 4.5 cm at center front and then baste an even bow out to both sides with a contrast color thread (it helps to make a template for

the neck shaping on newsprint and then you can mark the stitching line with tailor's chalk). Machine-stitch with zigzag along the basting line and then cut the neck opening ¼ in / .5 cm above the stitching. Pick up and knit 29 sts along the neck edge and set piece aside.

Three-Quarter Length Sleeves

With 2 strands of black held together, CO 57 (61) sts and work in ribbing for 1½ in / 4 cm as for lower edge of sweater. On last RS row, inc 4 sts evenly spaced across and then purl back. Inc by lifting strand between 2 sts, placing it on left ndl and then working k1f&b into loop = 2 new sts = 61 (65) sts. Add white and work in two-color brioche until sleeve measures approx 12¾ in / 32 cm or desired length.

BO 4 sts at each side at beg of the 4th and then 1st pattern rows.

Now work raglan shaping as for front/back. *At the same time*, when sleeve cap measures 4¼ (5¼) in / 11 (13) cm = 44 (52) rows, mark the center purl st. Dec around the 2 knit sts on each side of the marked purl st as for the raglan "seams" on every 12th row a total of 3 times. Finish by placing the rem 9 sts on a holder. Make other sleeve the same way.

Finishing

Sew the side, sleeve, and raglan seams with mattress st.

Pick up and knit stitches just under stitching line on front and pick up rem "live" sts of sleeves and back neck and place on a short circular, join to work in the round, and make a rolled rib collar (k1/p1) with black.

When neck measures 8¾ in / 22 cm, BO loosely. Fold collar to WS and sew down edge so that the sewing and seam lines are hidden.

Cap

The cap is worked back and forth on a circular ndl and seamed at the back.

With 2 strands of black Isager Alpaca 2 and short circular, CO 99 sts. Always knitting the first and last sts on every row, work in k1/k1 ribbing for 4¾ in / 12 cm:
Row 1 (WS): K1, *p1, k1*; rep * to *to last 2 sts and end p1, k1.
Row 2 (RS): K1, *k1, p1*; rep * to * to last 2 sts and end with, k2.
On the last RS row, dec to 81 sts evenly spaced across by working the double dec described above 9 times so that the pattern will continue. Purl back. Add 2 strands white Tvinni and work in two-colored brioche (as for sweater) for about 4 in / 10 cm.
Now begin shaping the crown on RS (the black side); decreases are all worked on a pattern row 1:
K1, *k3tog, 13 brioche sts*; rep * to * across and end with 12 brioche sts in last repeat and then k1 for edge st = 5 double decreases. Repeat the decrease row on every 4th row 6 times, making sure that you decrease into the same line of stitches and the decreases align (see photo). There will be 2 fewer sts between each dec across the row. When 11 sts rem, cut yarn and pull tail through rem sts. Seam back of cap with mattress st, joining brioche section on the RS and ribbing from WS (the ribbed edge is folded under).

1970s

They all mixed together—Hollywood starlets, artists, playboys in their smoking jackets, Little Italy's Mafioso, and black disco queens from Harlem. The cream of the New York jet set stood side by side with a huge crowd of hopeful and budding stars in line at the newly opened night club, Studio 54. Before long everyone was locked in behind the doorway's purple velvet curtains that marked the boundary between the graceless light of the everyday and the night's Promised Land where the disco rhythms exploded in a pulsating swirl of sweaty bodies and blinking disco lights. On a quiet May evening in 1978, the uncrowned queen of fashion, Bianca Jagger, arrived on a white horse led by a black pair without a stitch on her body and the paparazzi pictures of the young beauty's eccentric entrance flashed around the world. From one perspective, Studio 54 was not just any night club but a dream destination for the young, who danced on the waves of the flower power movement's sexual freedoms and rebellion against the establishment's restrictive norms. Clad in tight fitting jeans and flowing kaftan dresses the rich and famous covered themselves in a rustle of fabric and casually erotic styles. Right around the corner, however, loomed the hangover—AIDS in the 80's and straight career paths. But for that one blink of an eye, the only thing that existed was the rotation of the disco balls around a world of unconcerned pleasure.

CABLED VEST

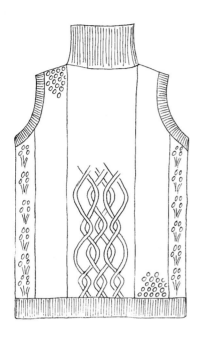 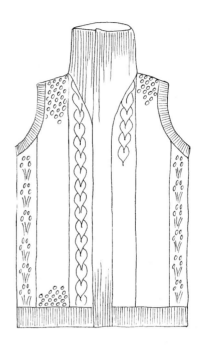

Sizes: S/M (M/L, L/XL)

Measurements
Chest: 39½ (45¾, 52) in / 100 (116, 132) cm
Sleeve length from underarm: 18½ in / 47 cm

Yarn
300 (350, 400) g Wool 1, color 1s (rust)
150 (200, 250) g Tvinni, color 33 (rust)
(you can substitute Isager Alpaca 2 for the
Tvinni)

Needles: US sizes 2.5, 4, and 9 / 3.0, 3.5
and 5.5 mm (2 dpn in each smaller size and
24 in / 60 cm circular of largest size); cable
needle.

Gauge
20 sts and 26 rows in k1/p1 ribbing (slightly
stretched) or cable/trinity pattern with 2
strands Wool 1 and 1 strand Tvinni held together on larger ndls = 4 x 4 in / 10 x 10 cm.
Adjust needle sizes to obtain correct gauge
if necessary.

Relief Stitch
On all RS rows, knit the relief st and on WS
rows, slip the st purlwise with yarn in front.

Patterns
Cable, trinity, and flower patterns are
explained on pages 60–61.

VEST

The vest is worked back and forth beginning at lower edge. The back and front are worked as one piece.

BACK AND FRONT

With 2 strands of Wool 1 and 1 of Tvinni held together and US 9 / 5.5 mm ndls, CO 211 (243, 275) sts and work in ribbing as follows:

Row 1 (WS): Sl 1 purlwise, *k1, p1*; rep * to * to last 2 sts and end k2.

Row 2 (RS): Sl 1 purlwise, *p1, k1*; rep * to * to last 2 sts and end p1, k1.

Repeat ribbing rows 1-2 for 2 in / 5 cm. Begin every row with sl 1 purlwise to form a chain edge along the fronts.

Now begin pattern knitting:

Row 1 and all odd-numbered rows (WS): Sl 1 purlwise, 11 sts k1/p1 ribbing, 1 relief st (= sl 1 purlwise wyf), 17 sts double cable, 1 relief st, 20 (28, 36) sts trinity pattern, 1 relief st, 16 sts flower pattern, 1 relief st, 20 (28, 36) sts trinity, 1 relief st, 32 sts large cable, 1 relief st, 20 (28, 36) sts trinity, 1 relief st, 16 sts flower, 1 relief st, 20 (28, 36) sts trinity, 1 relief st, 16 sts + m1 (= 17 sts; see Note) double cable, 1 relief st, 12 sts k1/p1 ribbing = a total of 212 (244, 276) sts.

Note: the m1 is made so that the pattern repeat works and the outermost edges will be alike.

Row 2 and all even-numbered rows (RS): Work in pattern as set. Don't forget that the relief sts are always knitted on RS.

The flower pattern is centered at each underarm. Each front has 60 (68, 76) sts and the back has 92 (108, 124) sts.

Continue in pattern until piece measures approx 10¾ in / 27 cm. If you want loops for the belt, work them into the 4 trinity sections as follows:

End on a WS pattern row. Using 1 strand each of Wool 1 and Tvinni and ndls US size 4 / 3.5 mm, pick up and knit 6 sts at the center of a trinity section (in front of existing sts on ndl). Work these sts in k1/p1 ribbing, increasing to 7 sts so the edge sts match at both sides:

Sl 1 purlwise, *k1, p1*; rep * to * to last st and end k1. Work in ribbing for 1½ in / 3.5 cm and then dec to 6 sts and place sts on a holder. Work the other 3 belt loops the same way.

Change back to main pattern, needles and yarn and continue until body is level with top of belt loops. Now work the sts of the loops together with the corresponding sts in the pattern.

Work in pattern until piece measures about 17¾ in / 45 cm, or desired length, and then begin shaping armhole. First BO the center 8 sts of the flower pattern at each side. Now work the back and each front separately.

FRONT

At armhole side of front, BO 3 sts. The rem st of flower pattern should now be an edge st (next to relief st) and always knitted. Continue shaping the armhole by decreasing within the trinity pattern inside the 2 edge sts, k2tog on both RS and WS rows a total of 2 times = 16 (24, 32) sts rem in trinity pattern. *Note:* Make sure that the patterns align.

When the piece measures approx 3¼ in / 8 cm from the first armhole dec, place the 2 x 11 ribbing sts of front on a stitch holder.

Now begin shaping V-neck by working k2tog inside the 2 outermost sts on every other row a total of 17 times (all the sts of the double cable have been eliminated). End by knitting the 2 relief sts tog.

At the same time, after 14 V-neck decreases (3 sts left to dec), shape shoulders with short rows:

SHORT ROWS:

Work until 6 (8, 10) sts rem; turn, yo and work back.

Work until 8 (12, 16) sts rem (do not count yo); turn, yo and work back.

Work until 6 (8, 10) sts rem (do not count yo); turn, yo and work back.

Place 22 (30, 38) shoulder sts on a holder and work the other side of front the same way, reversing shaping to match.

BACK

Continue in pattern, shaping armhole and short rows for shoulders as for front (working across from shoulder to shoulder). Place rem 34 back sts on a holder.

With RS facing RS, join shoulders with three-needle bind-off; knit each yarnover with the st next to it to avoid holes.

COLLAR

Place rem 12 sts of right front onto ndl and knit, pick up and knit 36 sts along side of neck (the "knot" edge). Place the 32 sts of back neck on ndl and knit, then pick up and knit 36 sts along other side of neck, knit 12 sts of left front. Work in k1/p1 ribbing as follows:

Begin on WS: Sl 1, *p1, k1*; rep * to * and end with p1, k1. Continue in ribbing until collar measures approx 5¼ in / 13 cm. BO in ribbing.

ARMHOLE BANDS

Pick up and knit about 72 sts around knot edge of armhole. Join and work around in k1/p1 ribbing for 1–1¼ in / 2.5–3 cm. BO in ribbing.

BELT

The belt is worked in double knitting on larger ndls and is about 1¼ in / 3 cm wide. With 1 strand each of Wool 1 and Tvinni held together, CO 12 sts.

Row 1: Sl 1 purlwise, *k1, sl 1 purlwise wyf*; rep * to * and end with k1.

Repeat this row until belt is about 63 in / 160 cm long. Sl 1, k2 tog to last st and end k1; BO.

PATTERN ABBREVIATIONS

cn = cable needle

1/1FK = Place 1 st on cn and hold in front, p1 and then k1 from cn.

1/1F = Place 1 st on cn and hold in front, k1 and then k1 from cn.

2/1FP = Place 2 sts on cn and hold in front, p1 and then k2 from cn.

1/1BP = Place 1 st on cn and hold in back, k1 and then p1 from cn.

1/1B = Place 1 st on cn and hold in back, k1 and then k1 from cn.

1/2BP = Place 1 st on cn and hold in back, k2 and then p1 from cn.

2/2F = Place 2 sts on cn in front, k2 and then k2 from cn.

2/2B = Place 2 sts on cn and hold in back, k2 and then k2 from cn

LARGE CABLE ON BACK OF VEST

Worked over 32 sts as follows:

Row 1 (WS): K4, p2, *k4, p4*; rep * to *
until 10 sts rem and end with k4, p2, k4.

Row 2: P4, *2/1FP, p2, 1/2BP*; rep * to *
until 4 sts rem, end p4.

Row 3 (and all other odd-numbered, WS,
rows): Knit over knit and purl over purl.

Row 4: P5, *2/1FP, 1/2BP, p2*; rep * to *
until 3 sts rem and end p3.

Row 6: P2, *p4, 2/2B*; rep * to * until 6 sts
rem and end p6.

Row 8: P5, *1/2BP, 2/1FP, p2*; rep * to *
until 3 sts rem and end p3.

Row 10: Work knit over knit and purl over
purl.

Row 12: P5, *2/1FP, 1/2BP, p2*; rep * to *
until 3 sts rem and end p3.

Row 14: P2, *p4, 2/2B*; rep * to * until 6 sts
rem and end p6.

Row 16: P5, *1/2BP, 2/1FP, p2*; rep * to *
until 3 sts rem and end p3.

Row 18: P4, *1/2BP, p2, 2/1FP*; rep * to *
until 4 sts rem and end p4.

Row 20: P3, 1/2BP, *p4, 2/2F*; rep * to *
until 10 sts rem and end p4, 2/1FP, p3.

Row 22: P2, 1/2BP, p4, *1/2BP, 2/1FP,
p2*; rep * to * until 7 sts rem and end p2,
2/1FP, p2.

Row 24: Work knit over knit and purl over
purl.

Row 26: P2, 2/1FP, p4, *2/1FP, 1/2BP,
p2*; rep * to * until 9 sts rem and end, p2,
1/2BP, p2.

Row 28: P3, 2/1FP, *p4, 2/2F*; rep * to *
until 10 sts rem and end p4, 1/2BP, p3.
Repeat these 28 rows.

TRINITY PATTERN

Worked over 20 (28, 36) sts:
Row 1 (WS): *(k1, p1, k1) in the same st,

p3tog*; rep * to *.
Row 2: Purl.
Row 3: *P3tog, (k1, p1, k1) into same st*;
rep * to *.
Row 4: Purl.
Repeat these 4 rows.

FLOWER PATTERN

Worked over 16 sts
Row 1 (WS): K7, p2, k7.
Row 2: P6, 1/1B, 1/1F, p6.
Row 3: K5, 1/1FK, p2, 1/1BP, k5.
Row 4: P4, 1/1BP, 1/1B, 1/1F, 1/1FK, p4.
Row 5: K3, 1/1FK, k1, p4, k1, 1/1BP, k3.
Row 6: p2, 1/1BP, p1, 1/1BP, k2, 1/1FK,
p1, 1/1FK, p2.
Row 7: (K2, p1) 2 times, k1, p2, k1, (p1, k2)
2 times.
Row 8: P2, make a bobble *on ndls US 2.5 / 3
mm* (k1, k1tbl) 2 times into next st; turn, p4,
turn, k4; turn, p2tog, p2tog; turn, k2tog —

bobble is now complete. Change back to US
9 / 5.5 mm ndls and continue: p1, 1/1BP, p1,
k2, p1, 1/1FK, p1, bobble, p2.
Row 9: K4, p1, k2, p2, k2, p1, k4.
Row 10: P4, bobble, p2, k2, p2, bobble, p4.
Repeat rows 1–10.

DOUBLE CABLE

Worked over 17 sts:
Row 1 and all odd-numbered, WS, rows:
K2, p6, k1, p6, k2.
Rows 2 and 4: P2, k6, p1, k6, p2.
Row 6: P2, place next 3 sts on cn behind
work, k3, k3 from cn, p1, place the next 3
sts on cn in front, k3, k3 from cn, p2.
Row 8: As for row 2.
Repeat rows 1–8 (cable is turned on every
8th row).

CHEVRON SCARF

Measurements

Width: 8¾ in / 22 cm
Length: 71 in / 180 cm

Yarn

About 50 g of 6 different colors of Highland,
Tvinni or Isager Alpaca 2.
For the scarf shown, we used:
Highland, color Plaster
Isager Alpaca 2, colors 015 (peach) and
017 (curry)
Tvinni, colors 1s (rust), 36 (plum), and
55 (eggplant)

Needles: US size 4 / 3.5 mm (straight).

Gauge

25 sts and 38 rows in garter st with 2 strands
held together = 4 x 4 in / 10 x 10 cm.
Adjust needle size to obtain correct gauge if
necessary.

Make 1 increase (m1)

Lift strand between 2 sts onto left ndl and
knit into back loop.

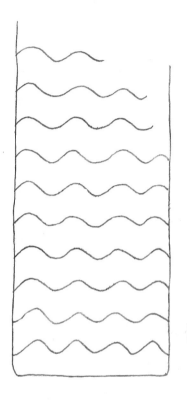

SCARF

With 1 strand each Highland plaster and Alpaca 2 (peach) held together, CO 4 sts and make a triangle:

TRIANGLE:

Row 1 and all other odd-numbered rows: Knit.

Row 2: K1, m1, k2, m1, k1.

Row 4: K1, m1, k1, m1, k2, m1, k1, m1, k1.

Row 6: K1, m1, k3, m1, k2, m1, k3, m1, k1.

There should now be 14 sts.

Cut yarn and make another triangle next to the first one. Make a total of 4 triangles the same way.

CO 1 st (edge st), knit across sts of all 4 triangles (56) sts, CO 1, and then work in chevron pattern (see color sequence below):

Row 1: Sl 1 purlwise, *k2tog, k3, m1, k2, m1, k3, ssk, k2*. Rep * to * and end with k1 instead of k2.

Row 2: Sl 1 purlwise and then knit rem sts across.

Rep these 2 rows changing colors every 2 in / 5 cm in this color sequence:

When piece measures 2 in / 5 cm, use Isager Alpaca 2 curry instead of plaster.

Every 2 in / 5 cm, make these changes: Tvinni rust instead of Alpaca 2 peach, Tvinni plum instead of Isager Alpaca 2 curry, Tvinni eggplant instead of Tvinni rust.

After a sequence ends with the darkest color, change back to a slightly lighter color and work with increasingly lighter colors until using the lightest color again and then repeat sequence—light to dark and dark to light.

When scarf is about 71 in / 180 cm long and you've knitted 2 in /5 cm with the 2 lightest colors, finish with half triangles:

First half triangle:

K1, k2tog, k4; turn.

Sl 1 purlwise, k1, psso, k4, turn.

K1, k2tog, k2; turn.

Sl 1 purlwise, k1, psso, k2.

K1, k2tog; turn, sl 1 purlwise, k1, psso.

Cut yarn and pull tail through rem st.

Whole triangles 1, 2, and 3:

K2, pass 1st over 2nd, k2, k2tog, k2, k2tog, k4; turn, sl 1 purlwise, k1, psso, k9; turn.

Sl 1 purlwise, k1, psso, k2tog, k2, k2tog, k2; turn.

Sl 1 purlwise, k1, psso, k2tog, k2tog, k1; turn.

Sl 1 purlwise, k1, psso, sl 1, k1, psso. Cut yarn and work the next 2 triangles the same way.

Last half triangle:

K2, pass 1st st over 2nd, k5; turn.

K1, k2tog, k3; turn.

Sl 1 purlwise, k1, psso, k3; turn.

K1, k2tog, k1; turn.

Sl 1 purlwise, k2tog, psso. Cut yarn and weave in all tails on WS.

Finish by steam pressing scarf under a damp pressing cloth.

Child's Honeycomb Sweater

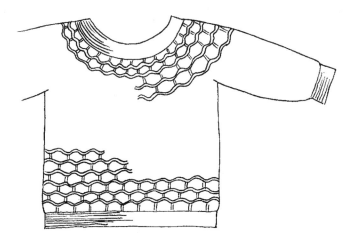

Sizes: 6 months–1 year (2–3 years, 4–5 years)

Measurements

Chest: 21¾ (24, 26½) in / 55 (61, 67) cm
Length below underarm: 8 (9½, 11) in / 20
(24, 28) cm
Total length: 12¾ (13¾, 15) in / 32 (35, 38) cm
Sleeve length from neckline: 10¾ (11¾,
14¼) in / 27 (30, 36) cm

Yarn

Color A (MC): 100 (100, 100) g Isager
Alpaca 2, color 011 (dark blue)
Color B (pattern): Small amounts (about
10 g each) of 7–9 different colors of Tvinni,
Wool 1, Highland or Isager Alpaca 2. Any
and all colors can be used and the result will
be fantastic even if the colors don't match.
We used these colors for the sweater shown:
Isager Alpaca 2 colors 012 (gray-green),
014 (orange), 015 (peach), 016 (lime), 017
(curry), 019 (ice blue), 020 (petroleum);
Tvinni colors 32s (red) and 36 (plum)

Notions: Small button for neckband.

Needles: US sizes 2.5 and 4 / 3 and 3.5 mm
(16 in / 40 cm circulars and dpn).

Gauge

26 sts and 47 rows in honeycomb pattern on
larger ndls = 4 x 4 in / 10 x 10 cm.
24 sts and 56 rows in garter st on smaller
ndls = 4 x 4 in / 10 x 10 cm.
Adjust needle sizes to obtain correct gauge
if necessary.

The sweater is worked in the round beginning
at lower edge.

BACK AND FRONT

With color B and smaller circular, CO
136 (152, 168) sts, join, being careful not
to twist cast-on row. Work in garter st in
the round (= alternate 1 knit rnd and 1 purl
rnd), for 1¼ in / 3 cm, changing colors on
every rnd. On the last rnd, inc evenly spaced
around (= m1 after every 17th (19th, 21st) st)
to 144 (160, 176) sts. You should now have
the correct stitch count for 18 (20, 22) rep
of honeycomb pattern (pattern is a multiple
of 8 sts).

Change to larger circular and honeycomb
pattern:
Rnd 1, with B: Knit.
Rnd 2, with B: Purl.
Rnds 3–8, with A: *Sl 2 purlwise wyb (= 2
relief sts), k6*; rep * to * around.
Rnds 9 and 11, with B: Knit.
Rnds 10 and 12, with B: Purl.
Rnds 13–18, with A: K4, *sl 2 purlwise wyb,
k6*; rep * to * around until 4 sts rem and end
sl 2 purlwise wyb, k2.
Rnd 19, with B: Knit.
Rnd 20, with B: Purl.
Repeat rnds 1–20 until piece measures 8
(9½, 11) in / 20 (24, 28) cm (= 8 (10, 12)
blocks). The pattern will work out well and
be straight across if you end with 2 ridges.

Mark sides so you have two sections with 9
(10, 11) blocks in each; set body aside.

SLEEVES

The sleeves are worked in the round on dpn.
With smaller dpn and B, CO 36 (42, 48)
sts and work in garter st as for lower edge of
body. When cuff measures 1¼ in / 3 cm, inc
evenly spaced around (= m1 after every 6th
(7th, 8th) st to 42 (48, 54) sts = stitch count
for 7 (8, 9) pattern rep (*Note:* stitch count
for sleeve honeycomb pattern begins as a
multiple of 6 sts). Change to larger dpn and
honeycomb pattern below.
Note: Begin size 6 months–1 year on rnd 1;
sizes 2–4 and 4–5 years begin on rnd 11.
Make sure that the stitch count stays constant.

Rnd 1, with B: Knit.
Rnd 2, with B: Purl.
Rnds 3–8, with A: *Sl 2 purlwise wyb (= 2
relief sts), k4*; rep * to * around.
Rnds 9 and 11, with B: Knit.
Rnds 10 and 12, with B: Purl.
Rnds 13–18, with A: K3, *sl 2 purlwise wyb,
k4*; rep * to * around until 3 sts rem and end
sl 2 purlwise wyb, k1.
Rnd 19, with B: Knit.
Rnd 20, with B: Purl.
Repeat rnds 1–20.

When honeycomb section measures approx
2¼ in / 5.5 cm (in the 3rd honeycomb), inc
1 st with m1 at the center of each block so
each now has 5 sts and the stitch count is 49
(56, 63) total. Continue in pattern for another
2¼ in / 5.5 cm and inc the same way on the
6th row of blocks = 6 sts in each block and
stitch count is 56 (64, 72) sts. Make sure
that the pattern stays consistent so that the
blocks are staggered as before. Continue in
pattern until sleeve measures 7 (8, 9½) in / 18
(20, 24) cm = 8 (9, 11) blocks in length.

Set sleeve aside and work the other one the
same way.

YOKE

Place a sleeve, front, sleeve, and back on larger circular and work around in pattern on all 256 (288, 320) sts. For size 4–5 years, work a half pattern rep = 1 block in length before decreasing. On the next block in length, work k2tog at the center of each block around so that the stitch count is now 224 (252, 280) (= 32 (36, 40) sts dec), and there are 5 sts in each block. Make sure that the pattern blocks are staggered as before. Rep this dec on the next complete row of blocks so there are now 4 sts in each block and 192 (216, 240) sts rem. Continue in pattern, decreasing the blocks a total of 4 times (= 2 sts rem within each block) and sweater measures approx 4 (4, 4¾) / 10 (10, 12) cm from underarm. When you complete the repeats, 128 (144, 160) sts rem.

End with 1¼ (1½, 1¼) in / 3 (4, 3) cm in garter st for neckband. Cut yarn and move the sts so that the rnd begins at the center back; change to smaller circular. Work back and forth (knit every row), always slipping the first st of every row purlwise; knit 2nd st on RS and and sl it wyf on WS.
At the same time, with k2tog, dec 16 (18, 20) sts evenly spaced across = k3, (k2tog, k6) 15 (17, 19) times and end k2tog, k3 = 112 (126, 140) sts rem. On every 4th row, dec 12 (14, 15) sts evenly spaced across a total of 3 times = 76 (84, 95) sts rem. Work one last dec row (dec 12, 14, 15 sts as before), and, BO at the same time, making sure that the bind off is not too tight.
For size 2-4 years, finish as follows: Work an extra ⅜ in / 1 cm in garter st and decrease 6 sts evenly spaced across the last row at the same time as you bind off.

Finish by sewing a button loop to the top of the neckband and sew a small button to the opposite side. Weave in all tails neatly on WS and then steam press sweater on WS under a damp pressing cloth.

1980s

"Discipline is freedom." This motto echoed among 17 million women worldwide who had bought the actress and fitness guru Jane Fonda's latest workout video. The video played on VHS, the latest technological wonder. After they sweated on the floor in the fight for the perfect body—an advanced and controlled machine—they could slide into fashion's revolutionary *power suit*, which, with its voluminous shoulder pads and narrow hips, mimicked a powerful man's Wall Street uniform. Self control was the codeword. Success became the goal of every career line and the youthful "haves" flashed their designer jeans, gold cards and designer bags on the streamlined floors of the night clubs' cold steel and neon colored plastic. The young Urban Professionals, soon dubbed *yuppies*, were the era's invincible personalities. Their cynical goal setting and status fixated lifestyle was portrayed in pop culture film and literature. But even if the body can be tamed, the machine isn't invincible. The new illness AIDS created frightening headlines although, when it was first designated as a pandemic, the middle class thought it wouldn't infect them even if the American President, Ronald Reagan, called it "the people's enemy number one." In the meantime the media-bombarded teenage generation drank Diet Coke, twined fingers in dark cinemas and shouted uncomfortably to Madonna's hit "Like a Virgin" on MTV.

> Self control was the codeword. Success became the goal of every career line and the youthful "haves" flashed their designer jeans, gold cards and designer bags on the streamlined floors of the night clubs' cold steel and neon colored plastic

LACE BLOUSE

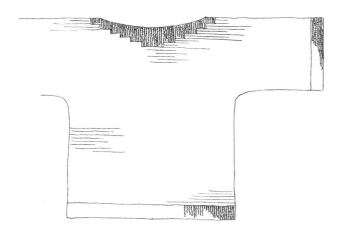

Sizes: S/M (M/L)

Measurements
Chest: 43¼ (46½) in / 110 (118) cm
Sleeve length: 11 (11¾) in / 28 (30) cm
Total length: 25½ (26¾) in / 65 (68) cm
Neck width: 11¾ in / 30 cm

Yarn
250 (300) g Isager Alpaca 2, color 100
(natural white)

Needles: US sizes 2.5 and 4 / 3 and 3.5 mm
(straight ndls)

Gauge
24 sts and 40 rows in lace pattern on larger
ndls = 4 x 4 in / 10 x 10 cm.
26 sts and 50 rows in garter st on smaller
ndls = 4 x 4 in / 10 x 10 cm.
Adjust needle sizes to obtain correct gauge
if necessary.

The blouse is knit in one piece from sleeve to
sleeve. The sleeves and sides are seamed in
finishing.
Please read through the entire pattern *before*
you begin knitting.

BLOUSE

With smaller ndls and 1 strand Isager Alpaca 2 yarn, CO 122 sts and work lower edge in garter st:

Row 1 (WS): Knit across.

Continue in garter st (knit across) until edge measures 1½ in / 4 cm. End with a WS row. Change to larger ndls and lace pattern:

Row 1 (RS): K1, *k2, yo, k2tog*. Rep from * to * and end with k1.

Repeat this row until the piece measures 11 (11¾) in / 28 (30) cm from beginning.

CO 4 new sts at the end of each of the next 8 rows, and work the new sts into pattern. Don't forget that the outermost st should always be knit ("knot" edge st). The stitch count is now increased by 16 sts at each side = 154 sts.

CO 76 (83) sts at the end of the next 2 rows = 306 (320) sts total. Continue working these sts in pattern as set but work a garter st edging with the outermost 11 sts at each side as follows:

RS: Sl 1 purlwise, k10, work in pattern until 11 sts rem, end k11.

WS: Sl1 purlwise, sl1 purlwise wyf (= relief st), work in pattern until 11 sts rem, end k9, sl 1 purlwise wyf, k1.

This method of working makes a nice chain edge as a finishing.

When piece measures 13¾ (14½) in / 35 (37) cm, begin garter st around the neckline. Work 149 (156) sts in pattern as before, k8, work 149 (156) sts in pattern. This should work with an even number of knit sts on each side of the vertical stripe lying at the center of the piece. Work the same way for 14 rows (= 7 ridges), with the pattern worked as previously.

Now shape neckline. Divide the piece at the center and work each half separately with 4 garter sts at the neck edge.

Shape neckline motif by increasing the number of garter sts by 4 on every 14 rows a total of 5 times (that is, change 4 pattern sts to garter sts; see detail photo on p. 75).

At the same time, round the neckline with k2tog inside the 2 outermost sts on every 6th row a total of 8 times.

After having decreased a total of 8 times, there should be 16 garter sts at neck. Work a total of 28 rows without decreasing, with 16 garter sts at neck and rem sts in lace pattern. After 14 rows, mark the center of the neck shaping with a thread or marker. From this point, the patterning and shaping is reversed. Begin by increasing with m1 inside the 2 edge sts after the total 28 rows (= 14 rows after the center point) have been knitted.

At the same time, work 4 more sts in lace pattern, so that the garter neck edge is reversed. When 4 garter sts rem, and the neck edge measures about 11¾ in / 30 cm across, set piece aside (= front of blouse). Work the back side of the blouse the same way shaping neckline to match front. When back has the same number of rows as the front, place all the sts on a needle. Now work the other side of the blouse to match the first side, binding off sts where you had previously cast on.

Steam press the garment under a damp cloth and finish by seaming side and sleeves with mattress st. BO loosely.

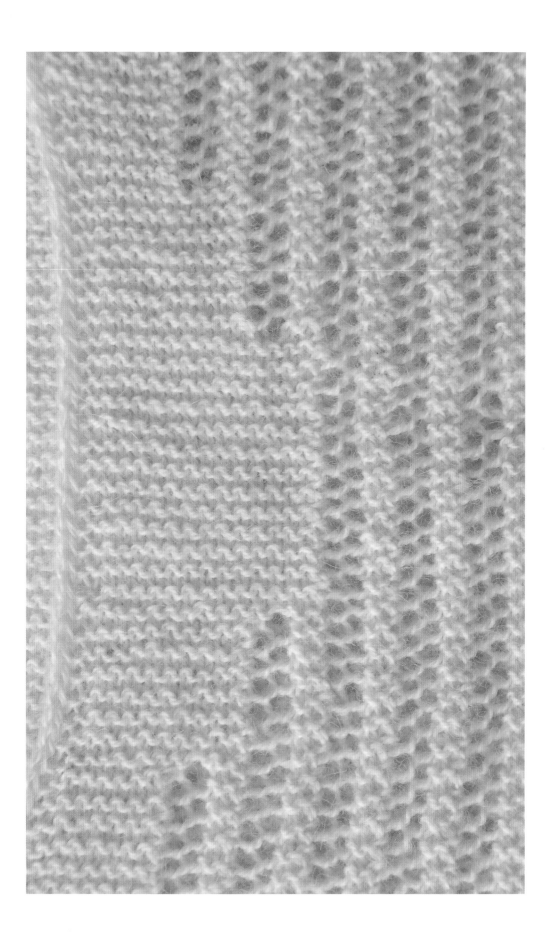

Neck and Leg Warmers

Size: One size

Measurements:
Neck Warmer:
Circumference: 22¾ in / 58 cm
Length: 11 in / 28 cm

Leg Warmers:
Length: 20½ in / 52 cm

Yarn
Neck Warmer:
50 g Highland, color Plaster
50 g Isager Alpaca 1, color 100 (natural white)
50 g Isager Alpaca 2, color 2105 (light gray)

Leg Warmers:
100 g Highland, color Plaster
50 g Isager Alpaca 1, color 100 (natural white)
100 g Isager Alpaca 2, color 2105 (light gray)

Needles: US sizes 6 and 7 / 4 and 4.5 mm
(straight and dpn)

Notions: 4 buttons (approx 5/8 in / 1.5 cm
diameter) for neck warmer

Gauge:
19 sts and 26 rows in 3/3 ribbing with 1
strand of each yarn held together on larger
needles = 4 x 4 in / 10 x 10 cm.
22 sts and 26 rows in 2/2 ribbing with 1
strand of each yarn held together on smaller
needles = 4 x 4 in / 10 x 10 cm.

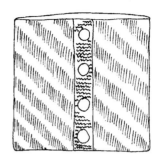

Neck Warmer

With larger ndls and 1 strand of each yarn held together, CO 109 sts and work back and forth in diagonal rib:

Row 1 (WS): Sl1 purlwise, sl 1 purlwise wyf (= 1 relief st), k5, sl 1 wyf, *k3, p3*. Rep from * to * until 11 sts rem and end with k3, sl 1 wyf, k5, p1, k1.
Row 2: Sl 1 purlwise, k8, *p3, k3*. Rep from * to * until 13 sts rem and end with k3, p2, k8.
Row 3: Sl 1 purlwise, sl 1 wyf, k5, sl1 wyf, k2, *p3, k3*. Rep * to * until 12 sts rem and end with k3, p1, sl 1 wyf, k5, sl 1 wyf, k1.
Row 4: Sl 1 purlwise, k9, *p3, k3*. Rep * to * until 9 sts rem and end with p1, k8.
Row 5: Sl 1 purlwise, sl 1 wyf, k5, sl 1 wyf, k1, *p3, k3*. Rep * to * until 13 sts rem and end with k3, p2, sl 1 wyf, k5, sl 1 wyf, k1.
Row 6: Sl 1 purlwise, k10, *p3, k3*. Rep * to * until 11 sts sts rem and end with k11.

Continue the same way, shifting the rib on RS by 1 st on every other row. The first and last 8 sts of each row are the button/buttonhole bands and are worked the same way throughout.

At the same time, after completing 5 ridges on edging, make a buttonhole on RS:
Sl 1 purlwise, k3, BO 2 sts and finish row as usual. On the next row (WS), CO 2 new sts over gap.

Continue in pattern, making buttonholes spaced about 2 in / 5 cm apart. When piece measures 9¾ in / 25 cm, BO loosely in pattern on RS.

Weave in all yarn tails neatly on WS and sew on buttons.

Leg Warmers

With smaller ndls and 1 strand of each yarn held together, CO 42 sts and work back and forth in ribbing as follows:
Row 1 (WS): K1, p1, *k2, p2*. Rep * to * until 2 sts rem and end with p1, k1.
Row 2: *K2, p2*. Rep * to * and end with k2.
Repeat these 2 rows until rib measures 6 in / 15 cm.

Change to dpn US size 7 / 4.5 mm and increase evenly to 60 sts by increasing with m1 in the ribs so that the ribs are now k3, p3 around. When increasing, take into account that the "knot" edge sts (knit st at each side to be used for seaming later) should be reduced with k2tog to 1 st which can be worked into the pattern so that there are 20 rib stripes where there were previously 21.

Join to work ribbing in the round (k3, p3) and shift the ribbing by 1 st on every other rnd as described in pattern for Neck Warmer.

When leg warmer measures about 17¾ in / 45 cm, change to smaller dpn and continue in the rnd (k3, p3) ribbing for about 3¼ in / 8 cm without shifting the rib pattern. BO evenly in ribbing and weave in all tails neatly on WS. Make the other leg warmer the same way.

Seam the leg warmers over the lower 2½ in / 6 cm of the ribbing, leaving the rest open over the heel.

1990s

The new sound sent shockwaves through a rootless generation of youth, who were united by songs from the world's new musical power center on the west coast of the U.S. Seattle was the city they listened to. This new, rough, and unpolished style, quickly christened *grunge,* was the long-awaited soundtrack for a generation that had grown up with their parents' middle class comforts in the big city's endless suburbs. But, instead of rebelling, these young people shuffled restlessly between MTV, McJobs and the truth at the bottom on a beer can—always keeping an ironic distance to life. Everything was confused in a flickering media-saturated reality. Kurt Cobain stood at the center of this musical scene. His band Nirvana hit a quivering nerve of the '90's and he became his generation's reluctant hero. In sync with the melody's noisy guitar riffs from the hit "Smells Like Teen Spirit" the noise also signaled the beginning of the lionized musician's self destruction. The world's camera lenses focused on an atypical idol, whose distinguishing high point of fame was dissolution. He tried to end it all during a tour in Paris with a cocktail of champagne and antidepressants. Just a month later, he succeeded. Kurt Cobain was found dead of a single shot to the head in his garage in Seattle on the morning of April 8, 1994. He was only 27 years old.

> This new, rough, and unpolished style, quickly christened *grunge,* was the long-awaited soundtrack for a generation that had grown up with their parents' middle class comforts in the big city's endless suburbs

DROP STITCH SWEATER

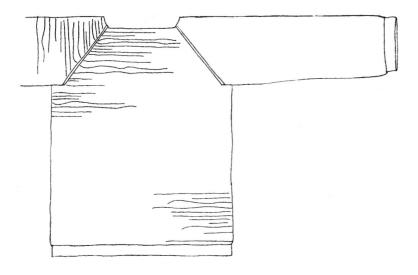

Sizes: S/M (M/L)

Measurements

Chest: 36¼ (39½) in / 92 (100) cm
Half neck width: 7 (7) in / 18 (18) cm
Body length below underarm: 16½ (17¼) in /
42 (44) cm
Total length: 24 (25½) in / 61 (65) cm
Sleeve length from underarm: 16½ (17¼) in /
42 (44) cm
Width, top of sleeve: 14¼ (15) in / 36 (38) cm

Yarn

450 (500) g total of the following yarns and
colors but you can also use small amounts of
what is on hand.

50 g Wool 1, colors 7s (light brown), 13s
(gray), 23s (gray-green)
50 g Isager Alpaca 2, colors 100 (natural
white), 201 (beige), 408 (camel)
100 g Isager Alpaca 2, colors 012 (gray-
green), 2105 (light gray)

Needles: US size 7 / 4.5 mm (24 in / 60 cm
circular and dpn) and US 9 / 5.5 mm (16
and 24 in / 40 and 60 cm circulars + dpn).

Gauge

13 sts and 20 rows in dropped stitch pattern
with larger ndls and 1 strand Wool 1 + 2
strands Alpaca 2 held together = 4 x 4 in /
10 x 10 cm.
15 sts and 36 rows in garter st with smaller
ndls and 1 strand Wool 1 + 2 strands Alpaca
2 held together = 4 x 4 in / 10 x 10 cm.
Adjust needle sizes to obtain correct gauge
if necessary.

The idea behind this sweater is that the
knitter will experiment with colors, materials, and pattern so that the overall effect is a
rather unstructured, random expression. Of
course, though, it is important that correct
gauge be maintained and the sweater shaped
as indicated so that it will fit properly.

The sweater is worked from the top down.
Hold 3 strands of yarn together; for example,
2 strands of Alpaca 2 + 1 strand of Wool 1.

Sweater

With 1 strand Wool 1 and 2 strands Isager Alpaca 2 held together and larger 16 in / 40 cm circular (*Note:* change to longer circular when possible), CO 64 sts; join, being careful not to twist cast-on row. K22, pm, p2, pm (the 2 purl sts = raglan seam), k6, pm, p2, pm, k22, pm, p2, pm, k6, pm, p2, pm.

On every other rnd, m1 on each side of the 4 sets of purled/marked sts until raglan seam measures approx 8¾ (9½) in / 22 (24) cm. *To begin raglan shaping:* (K22, m1, sl marker, p2, slip marker, m1, k6, m1, sl marker, p2, slip marker, m1) 2 times. There will be 2 more sts on body/sleeves between markers after each inc rnd = 8 sts added per inc rnd.

At the same time, work patterning as, for example: 4 rnds stockinette; cut Isager Alpaca 2 and join another color of Isager Alpaca 2 and then purl 1 rnd.

Now work in pattern with horizontal dropped stitches:
K1, yo, k1, yo, k1, yo, k1, yo 2 times, k1, yo, k1, yo, k1, yo, k1 (= 8 sts + yarnovers), work 29 sts and repeat dropped stitch pattern (= *-*). Knit 1 rnd and then, on the next rnd, let all the yarnovers slide off the ndl, knitting the knit sts between them. *Don't forget to continue raglan shaping at the same time.*

Change color and yarn and then purl 3 rnds. Change color and yarn and knit 2 rnds. Work 1 rnd with dropped sts placed randomly.

Try on the sweater to make sure the fit to underarm is correct. Add or remove rounds as necessary. After finishing the raglan shaping, place the sleeve sts + 1 st from each raglan seam onto holders and CO 5 sts at each underarm. Continue around in pattern with the sts of back and front. Work in pattern until sweater is about 15½ (16¼) in / 39 (41) cm down from underarm. Change to smaller circular and work 6 ridges in the round: alternate 1 knit and 1 purl rnd = 12 rnds. BO (be careful not to bind off too tightly).

Sleeves

Place sts of one sleeve onto larger size short circular and then pick up and knit 7 sts from underarm (7 rather than 5 sts to avoid holes). Join and continue around in pattern. When you've worked approx 4 (3¼) in / 10 (8) cm on sleeve, k2tog at each side of center underarm stitch (= 2 sts dec). Rep this dec every 4 (3¼) in / 10 (8) cm 3 (4) times = 8 (10) sts dec total. Change to dpn when sts no longer fit around short circular. When sleeve measures 15½ (16¼) in / 39 (41) cm or desired length, change to smaller dpn and work 12 rnds (= 6 ridges) in garter st (alternate knit and purl rnds as for lower edge of body. BO. Work other sleeve the same way. Weave in all tails neatly on WS.

Yarn

Yarns used in this book

Highland
100% Merino wool
50 g = 308 yds / 280 m

Isager Alpaca 1
100% baby alpaca
50 g = 440 yds / 400 m

Isager Alpaca 2
50% alpaca, 50% Merino wool
50 g = 275 yds / 250 m

Wool 1
100% Merino wool
50 g = 340 yds / 310 m

Tvinni
100% Merino wool
100 g = 560 yds / 510 m

Viscolin
50% viscose, 50% linen
50 g = 203 yds / 185 m

All yarns distributed in the U.S. by
TUTTO Opal-Isager
10 Domingo Road
Santa Fe, NM 87508
www.knitisager.com

Recommended Tools

Knitting needles
bamboo or birch

Stitch holders
useful for holding
live stitches to be
set aside until needed later

Tape measure
used to check gauge
to make sure it is correct

Soft towel
cover with blocking
cloth (marked with grid
for measurements) when
blocking knit pieces

Pins
used to pin out gauge
swatches and completed
knit pieces

Small scissors
to cut threads with

Blunt tapestry needle
for seaming and weaving
in yarn ends

Worth Knowing

Blocking Knitted Pieces

Before sewing a knitted garment together, you should wet and pin-block it. Blocking makes the seaming easier and improves the look of the garment.

Begin blocking by soaking the knitted pieces in cold water. Lightly squeeze out the water and then roll the piece(s) in a towel to absorb the excess water. You can also block by lightly steam pressing the pieces under a damp pressing cloth.

Lay the pieces out on a carpet or blocking mat and pin out them to correct measurements. Let everything dry completely before removing pins.

You should always block gauge swatches the same way so you can be sure that you have the correct finished gauge.

Washing Knitwear

Woolens should be washed by hand in cold water but, if your washing machine has a delicate wool program, you can machine-wash in cold water. If you want to avoid felting the finished garment, it is important not to use too much soap. Use a good quality wool wash or mild hair shampoo. It is very important that the water temperature be consistent from the wash through all the rinses.

Once the garment has been washed and rinsed (avoid wringing the water out of the garment), you can place the garment in a nylon net washing bag and spin the water out in the machine or a centrifuge. Now lay the garment flat on towels and let it dry completely.

It isn't necessary to wash knitwear very often. Usually you can just air out the garment outside on a humid day.

Abbreviations

BO	bind off
CO	cast on
cm	centimeter(s)
cn	cable needle
dec	decrease
dpn	double-pointed needles
g	gram(s)
in	inch(es)
inc	increase
k	knit
k1f&b	knit into front and then back of the same stitch
k2tog or k3tog	knit 2 (or 3) together
k2tog tbl	knit 2 together through back loops (or work as ssk)
m	meter(s)
m1	make 1 = lift strand between two stitches and knit into back loop
MC	main color
mm	millimeter(s)
ndl(s)	needles
p	purl
pm	place marker
psso	pass slipped stitch over
rem	remain(ing)
rep	repeat
rnd(s)	round(s)
RS	right side
sl	slip
ssk or sssk	slip 2 (3) sts knitwise to right ndl one at a time and then knit into back loops
st(s)	stitch(es)
WS	wrong side
wfb	with yarn in back
wyf	with yarn in front
yd(s)	yard(s)
yo	yarn over

KNITTING SCHOOL

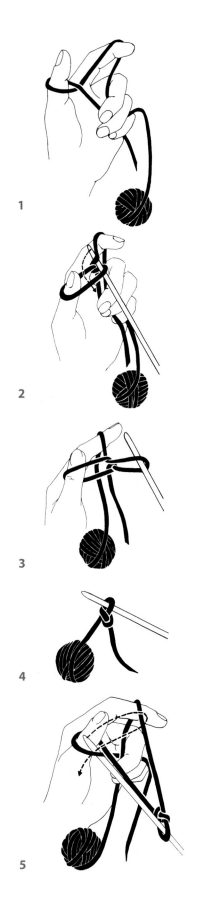

CASTING ON WHEN BEGINNING A PIECE

The method described here (long-tail cast-on) makes a secure and elastic edge. The first row will be easier to knit if you cast on over two needles held together.

1 Arrange the yarn as shown on the left hand with a loop of the yarn's free end around the thumb and a loop around the index finger with yarn from the ball. Be careful that the free end is long enough for the desired number of stitches to be cast on.

2 With your right hand, insert the needle through the thumb loop (needle goes under the front loop and over the back thumb loop) and then under the front loop on the index finger.

3 Use the needle to pull the new loop forward through the thumb loop and then slip loop off thumb.

4 The loop now around the right needle is the first stitch; tighten it a bit by pulling on the ends.

5 Now arrange the yarn around the thumb and index finger as in step 1 and make a new stitch by following steps 2–4. As you continue casting on new stitches the yarn stays on the index finger while, throughout, a new loop is made through the yarn tail over the thumb.

6 The drawings show the front (top drawing) and back (lower drawing) of this cast-on.

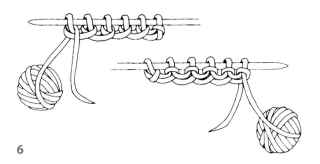

Casting On within the work

This method, a loop cast-on, is used when you are casting on new stitches, for example, for buttonholes.

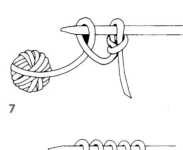

7

7 Cast on 1 st (see drawings 1–4). Hold the needle in the right hand. The stitch to the right is made from previously formed stitches. With the left hand, make a loop as shown in the drawing. Place the loop on the right needle and tighten slightly = 1 new stitch.

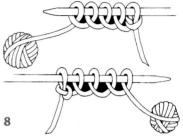

8

8 The drawing shows the front (top drawing) and back (lower drawing) of the loop cast-on.

Knit Stitches

Cast on stitches to begin the work (drawings 1–6).

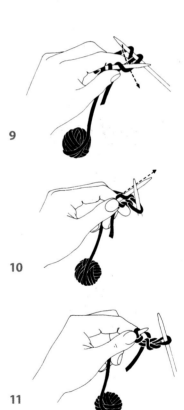

9

9 Hold the needle with the stitches in the left hand with the yarn coming from the ball over the index finger and with the last cast-on st at the front of left needle. Insert the right needle through the first stitch from below and left to right through the front "leg" of the loop. At this point, the needles point the same direction. Insert the right needle further back and over the yarn on the index finger. Pull the yarn down from the index finger and then forward through the stitch.

10

10 When the new loop is on the right needle, slide the old stitch off left needle.

11 A new stitch is now on the right needle. Continue the same way for the next stitch. When all of the stitches on the left needle have been knitted over to the right needle, turn the right needle, move it to the left hand and knit the next row as for the first.

11

12 The drawing shows garter stitch (all knit) over 8 stitches. It is worked the same way on both sides of the fabric.

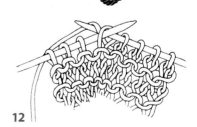

12

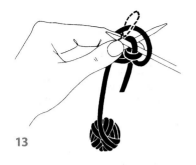

13

Purl Stitches and Stockinette

Cast on sts as for the beginning of a piece (drawings 1–6).

13 Hold the needle with the cast-on sts in the left hand with the last cast-on st at the front of the left needle and with the yarn from the ball over both left needle and index finger. Insert the right needle from behind, in under the yarn over the left needle and index finger and then through the first st loop, so that the two needles point towards each other. Insert the right needle back and over the index finger yarn.

14

14 Pull this loop down and back through the first st.

15 On the right needle, there is now a new stitch and the first st can be slipped off the left needle.

16 Purl the same way all across the row. The row facing you will look like garter stitch.

15

17 For stockinette, alternate 1 knit row with 1 purl row. The knit side is the right side (RS) and the purl is the wrong side (WS) for stockinette stitch.

Knitting in the round on a circular or on double-pointed needles

When you are knitting in the round, you always go in the same direction, beginning at the same side of the piece. By working in the round, you can knit all the rounds and avoid purling. Circular needles are available in 16, 24, 32, and 40 in / 40, 60, 80, 100 cm lengths. If there are too many stitches to go around even the smallest circular, you can use double-pointed needles instead.

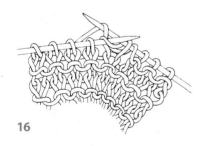

16

When working on double-pointed needles (dpn), evenly divide the sts over 3 or 4 needles and then knit with the 4th or 5th needle. Stitches worked on dpn can be a little loose when you change needles, so if you shift the sts regularly from needle to needle, then the change of needle is not always at the same place.

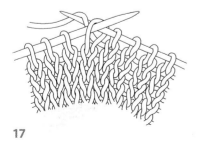

17

Short Rows

Short rows are used to form a gusset, for example, to shape shoulders or a dart. The drawings below illustrate short rows on both the right and wrong sides of the knitting.

18 Knit across RS until, for example, 4 sts remain; turn and then yarnover.

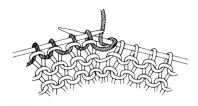

18

The yarnover is never counted as a stitch in short rows but is used to avoid a hole which would occur if you simply turned the work and knit back.

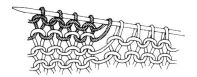

19

19 Purl back. You've now worked 2 rows higher at the left purl side and the yarnover can be seen at the turning hole.

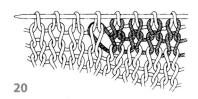

20 On the next RS (knit) row, work to the turning hole and then knit the yarnover with the first st after the hole.

20

21 On the WS, purl to the last 4 sts. Turn and yarnover.

22 Knit back. You've now completed 2 rows more on the left RS and the yarnover is visible at the turning hole.

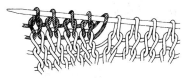

21

23 On the next purl (WS) row, work to the turning hole, and purl the yarnover through back loops with the first st after the hole.

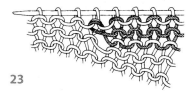

22

23

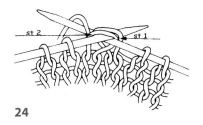

24

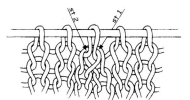

25

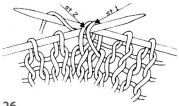

26

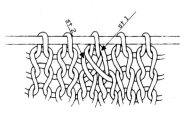

27

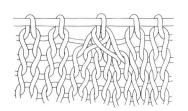

28

DECREASES

When you are decreasing around a marked stitch (or pair of stitches), for example a side or sleeve st, it looks best if the decreases slant towards each other. You can do this by knitting together through back loops (or ssk) before the marker and knitting 2 together after the marker.

KNIT 2 TOGETHER (K2TOG)

24 Generally you knit two together through both stitches.

25 The drawing shows how the 2nd st lies over the 1st st when the decrease is completed.

KNIT 2 TOGETHER THROUGH BACK LOOPS (K2TOG TBL)

26 Knit into the back of the 1st, then 2nd st.

27 The drawing shows that the 1st st lies over the 2nd st when this decrease has been worked.

DOUBLE DECREASE (SL1-K2TOG-PSSO)

28 Sl 1 st knitwise, knit 2 together (or purl if called for in pattern) and then slip the slipped st over the decrease.

The drawing shows how a completed double decrease looks.

Increase

When you need to add stitches to the knitting, it is called an increase. You can increase almost invisibly or with a hole.

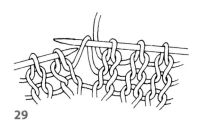

29

Hole increase

29 Lift the strand between two stitches onto the left needle and knit into front of it. This method of increase leaves a hole at that spot.

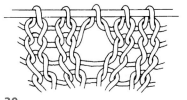

30

30 The completed increase seen from RS where you've made a new stitch and a hole at the same time.

Twisted Increase (m1)

31 Lift the strand between 2 stitches to left needle and knit into the back of the loop. The loop for the stitch is now twisted and won't leave a hole in the fabric.

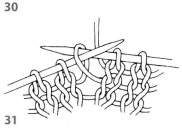

31

32 The completed increase seen from WS; the twist avoids a hole.

Two-color Brioche

33 Knit 1 through the stitch of row below.

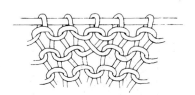

32

34 Purl 1 through the stitch of row below.

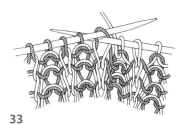

33

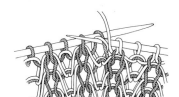

34

CABLES

A cable can be turned to the right or the left and made with just a few or several stitches. This cable shows 2 x 2 stitches twisted on each other.

35

LEFT-LEANING CABLE

35 Place the first two stitches for the cable onto a cable needle.

36

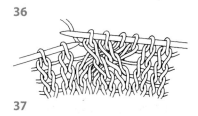

36 Hold the cable needle with the 2 sts in front of the work and then knit the next 2 sts.

37

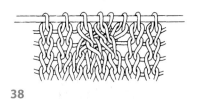

37 Now knit the 2 sts from the cable needle.

38 Work the remaining sts of the row.

38

RIGHT-LEANING CABLE

39 Place the first 2 stitches for the cable onto a cable needle and hold behind work.

39

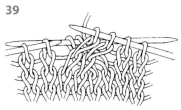

40 Knit the next 2 stitches.

41 Knit the 2 sts from cable needle.

40

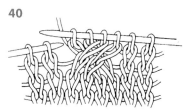

42 Complete rest of row.

41

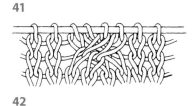

42

BINDING OFF (BO)

43 With right side facing, knit the first 2 sts. Insert the left needle into the 1st knitted st on right needle and then pull it over the last knit st on right needle. 1 st now remains on right needle and 1 stitch has been bound-off.

Knit 1 stitch and then slip the previously knit st over it. When all the sts have been bound-off and 1 st remains on right needle, cut the yarn and pull the tail through the stitch to finish it.

Make sure that you do not bind off too tightly. Make sure that the tension of the bound-off row matches that of the knitting.

44 Bound-off row as seen from RS.

45 Bound-off row as seen from WS.

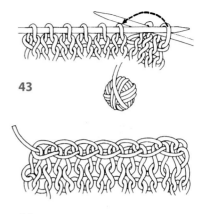

43

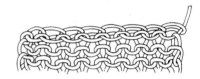

44

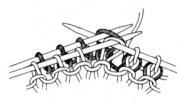

45

JOINING SETS OF STITCHES BY KNITTING TOGETHER AND/OR WITH THREE-NEEDLE BIND-OFF

When it is possible, it can be advantageous to join two pieces by knitting two sets of stitches together at the same time. For example, it is natural to knit 2 shoulders together so that the stitches will match from side to side and the joining makes a fine, elastic edge.

46

46 Place sts from one shoulder onto a needle and place the same number of stitches from the other shoulder onto another needle. Hold the 2 needles in the left hand with RS facing RS and then use a third needle to knit together the front stitch from each needle. Stitches can be bound off at the same time as joining (drawing 43) or you can bind off after the stitches have already been knit together.

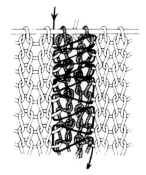

47

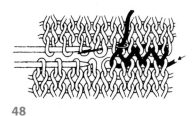

48

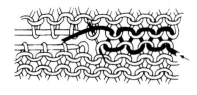

49

JOINING WITH MATTRESS STITCH

Mattress stitch is used for joining 2 vertical pieces of knitting, for example, a side or sleeve seam. For this join, it is good to have an edge stitch (always knit on both RS and WS). This type of outermost stitch is called a "knot" edge st.

47 The drawing of the stitch shows 2 pieces of stockinette with the right sides facing up and with the knot edge sts. It is sewn with RS facing using a back stitch. Insert needle behind the first row of stitches, that is, through the entire knot edge stitch. Alternately sew with backstitch through one side and then the other so that the needle in inserted down where it last came up.

JOINING WITH KITCHENER STITCH

Kitchener stitch joins 2 sets of live stitches still on the needles. This stitch exactly copies the route of a row of stitches and is therefore invisible.

There should always be the same number of stitches on each needle that will be joined with Kitchener. Use a blunt tapestry needle for the sewing.

48 The top drawing shows how to join 2 rows of stock-inette as seen from RS. The grafting yarn is black and, as can be seen, the yarn always goes into each stitch 2 times (except for the first and last stitches).

49 This drawing shows 2 rows of stockinette being joined on WS. The two needles, holding the sts in lace, are pulled out as the sewing proceeds.